BOATLIFE

Exploring the Freedom of Maritime Living

gestalten

Katharina Charpian

CONTENTS

SETTING A COURSE FOR FREEDOM 4

HAVING THE NORTHWESTERN MEDITERRANEAN COAST AS YOUR FRONT YARD
Mediterranean Sea | Feeling 1090 10

CHARTING A COURSE FOR CREATIVITY
Mediterranean Sea | Dufour 42 18

ONE COUPLE'S QUEST FOR CULTURE AND KITESURFING
Mediterranean Sea | Beneteau 49 26

MANY ROUTES LEAD INTO THE GREAT BLUE YONDER 38

FROM VAN-LIFE TO BOAT-LIFE
Mediterranean Sea & North Atlantic Ocean | Pearson 35 42

TAKING THE SLOW ROUTE TO HAWAII BY CATAMARAN
Mediterranean Sea & North Atlantic Ocean | Lagoon 380 S2 50

BETWEEN BUTTERFLIES AND SOUL FOOD IN THE TURKISH AEGEAN
Mediterranean Sea | Dufour 470 56

FROM SWEDEN TO THE CARIBBEAN AND BACK AS A MATURE GAP YEAR
North Atlantic Ocean & Caribbean Sea | Hanse 411 64

STEERING A COURSE BETWEEN RAYS AND REMOTE WORKING
North Atlantic Ocean, Caribbean Sea & Mediterranean Sea | Tayana 37 70

ZIGZAGGING THEIR WAY FROM THE U.K. TO GUADELOUPE
North Atlantic Ocean, Caribbean Sea & Mediterranean Sea | Contest 48CS 78

DIVING INTO AN ISLAND PARADISE 88

SAILING THE ROUTE LESS TRAVELED
North Atlantic Ocean | Buchanan Brabant 30,5 92

SAILING THE SCOTTISH HEBRIDES IN A CUTTER
North Atlantic Ocean & Irish Sea | Gaffel Cutter, 56 ft 102

A LIFE AT SEA IN PERPETUITY
North Atlantic Ocean | Concordia Yawl 41 108

CALIFORNIA DREAMING ABOARD A SELF-BUILT WOODEN CUTTER
Santa Barbara Channel | Self-made, inspired by James Cook 27 116

FOLLOWING THE "BAREFOOT ROUTE" FROM NORWAY TO NEW ZEALAND
South Pacific Ocean & North Atlantic Ocean | Beneteau Oceanis 40 124

ADVENTURES IN THE KINGDOM OF THE HUMPBACK WHALE
South Pacific Ocean | Tayana Vancouver 42 ... 132

LEARNING TO LIVE WITH LESS AT SEA ... 144

SAILING AMONG CORAL REEFS AND CROCODILES
Coral Sea | Concept 40 ... 148

FROM SOLO SAILOR TO ENVIRONMENTAL ACTIVIST
South Pacific Ocean | Cal 40 ... 156

FROM BRITISH COLUMBIA TO THE SHORES OF MEXICO
Salish Sea & Pacific Ocean | Tartan 42 ... 162

A FAMILY AND THEIR GREENLAND WILDERNESS ADVENTURE PLAYGROUND
Arctic Ocean & Norwegian Sea | Garcia 68 ... 172

MIDWINTER TO MIDSUMMER TO THE NORTH CAPE
Norwegian Sea | Beneteau First 345 ... 180

ADVENTURES IN THE LAND OF THE ORCAS, NORTHERN LIGHTS, AND SNOWY PEAKS
Norwegian Sea | Grand Soleil 46 ... 188

ADVENTURES BEYOND THE ARCTIC CIRCLE ... 198

CROSSING THE ARCTIC CIRCLE IN A CONVERTED LIFEBOAT
Norwegian Sea | Lifeboat, 38 ft ... 202

CONQUERING WILD WAVES TO GET TO "THE BIG ICE"
Southern Ocean & South Atlantic Ocean | Three-masted bark, 184 ft ... 208

VOYAGING THROUGH THE ICE TO THE CARIBBEAN
Arctic Ocean & North Atlantic Ocean | Bavaria 42 ... 220

GHOST TOWNS AND GLACIERS
Norwegian Sea & Arctic Ocean | Pearson 36 ... 230

MICRO-ADVENTURE IN A TINY SAILBOAT
Baltic Sea | Spaekhugger 24 ... 240

FROM SPEEDBOAT TO SELF-SUFFICIENT "SPACESHIP"
Havel River | Speedboat, 46 ft ... 248

INDEX ... 254

IMPRINT ... 256

SETTING A COURSE FOR FREEDOM

IMAGINE WAKING UP in a new anchorage every day, leaping straight from your boat's deck into crystal-clear waters, and beginning the day snorkeling through bright coral gardens, perhaps coming face to face with a turtle along the way. Just picture substituting working from home in the city to working from a floating office at sea and logging in to meetings with views of palm-fringed beaches as your backdrop. Fancy seeing the Northern Lights dancing over your mast amid the remote landscapes of the high latitudes? Or ascending a snow-covered peak straight from the boat with your skis and looking down to see a majestic humpback whale beside your floating home at anchor?

Those who opt for life on a boat will be surprised by adventures big and small every day. Some will be supremely challenging, others simply breathtaking—but they will invariably take you out of your comfort zone and boost your resilience. Instead of neatly fenced gardens or concrete monoliths, your home will be surrounded by the Seven Seas. In place of Netflix, you have the stars twinkling in the night sky and the vast blue expanse that covers over 70 percent of the Earth

and harbors a spectacular underwater realm. Your route is dictated not by steel rails, asphalt highways, or defined flight routes, but by the wind and the waves, which set the pace of day-to-day life. Only in a sailboat can you experience untrammeled nature out at sea in the most remote parts of the world or glide almost soundlessly over the wide Atlantic, with the glittering Milky Way overhead. Very few boat-lifers have a fixed route; they simply let themselves drift along, living in the moment.

Centuries ago, people discovered new continents by ship and passed down the tales of their adventures to their descendants. Between the 1950s and 1980s, the select group of solo round-the-world sailors were joined by a burgeoning movement of cruising sailors who left their old lives on terra firma behind and embarked on a new and thrilling chapter in their lives. They published tales of their exploits in travel diaries with titles like *Vagabond of the South Seas* (Bernard Moitessier) and *Two Girls, Two Catamarans* (James Wharram). Those accounts continue to inspire kindred spirits to this day and can be found in many an onboard library. Nevertheless, in those days, their authors were regarded as somewhat unconventional types—hippies of the sea.

Back then, the few crews that sailed full-time in the Caribbean, South Pacific, or Arctic Ocean seldom crossed paths and lacked any real means of communicating with new acquaintances at sea. By contrast, thanks to social media, today's boat-life community has a wealth of options for staying in touch, being visible, and inspiring others around the world with their lifestyle. Every day, more and more single people, couples, and groups of friends are moving onto sailboats, usually bought second-hand. They may take a sabbatical, leave city life behind for good, use a spell of parental leave to go on an epic trip, or embark on their new way of living with a digital job already in the bag. Barges, lifeboats, and speedboats are also being converted into mini floating apartments. Most boat-lifers do not have much experience, masses of cash to splash around, or thousands of nautical miles in their wake. Instead, this new generation lives by an ethos of "Just do it!" They want to start living their dreams and have decided that it is now or never.

Boat-life offers an opportunity to escape from rocketing property prices and energy costs that make a self-sufficient lifestyle especially appealing. Energy is provided by solar cells and wind generators, the wind in your vessel's sails propels you along, filter systems make seawater drinkable, and meals are served up by the ocean, rather than a delivery service. Those who live at sea tend to be more mindful of their environment and its resources, and travel with a very small environmental footprint.

Boat-life has some similarities to van-life, but some major differences, too. The two movements have evolved into global alternative living concepts geared towards minimalism. Camper vans and boats bring together people of different nationalities, ages, and professional backgrounds. But the boat-life scene also gives new meaning to the slow travel movement. While a van can average 60 mph (100 kph), a sailboat is more likely to glide sedately along at a tenth of the speed—no faster than a rickety old bicycle. Boat-lifers will find that it is not always possible to stop at the anchorage of their dreams—the wind, waves, water depth, and subsoil all have their say. Embracing boat-life means choosing independence at all levels and a life far removed from the services and comforts on tap in the West. Gas stations, supermarkets, medical clinics, and repair shops are often many nautical miles away. And for some, that is precisely what makes a self-determined, liberated life at sea so enticing. Instead of only experiencing the oceans from the coast, you get to immerse yourself in nature.

Two years ago, my boyfriend and I embarked on an Arctic voyage (page 180). At the time, I had absolutely no sailing experience, but I did manage to keep up with my job as a journalist while on board. Over time, I fell in love with our new lifestyle, and even though it would constantly push me to my limits, just a moment later it could bestow the most magical experiences on me. These emotional highs and lows are all part of life on the water, as the people featured in this book are only too aware. After our voyage, I said farewell to my city life in Hamburg. The two of us and our dog are currently exploring Europe's Atlantic coast in a 34 ft (10 m) sailboat—and that is just the start! After finishing this book, I want to cross oceans, see penguins from our pulpit, and traverse rivers in Africa. A much-cited quotation by the writer Horace Jackson Brown Jr. sums up exactly how I feel: "Twenty years from now you will be more disappointed by the things you didn't do than by the ones you did do. So throw off the bowlines. Sail away from the safe harbor. Catch the trade winds in your sails. Explore. Dream. Discover."

—Katharina Charpian

France
NORTH ATLANTIC
OCEAN
Corsica
Portugal
Spain
Balearic Islands
STRAIT OF GIBRALTAR
Morocco
Canary Islands
Algeria

Slovenia
Croatia
Bosnia
and Herzegovina
Italy
Albania
rdinia
Greece
Turkey
BLACK SEA
Sicily
nisia
MEDITERRANEAN
SEA
Cyprus
Lebanon
Israel
Libya
Egypt

HAVING THE NORTHWESTERN MEDITERRANEAN COAST AS YOUR FRONT YARD

DUNES AND SHORELINE FORESTS as well as lagoons, river islands, and rice paddies, with flamingos strutting through the marshland in between—you would not necessarily associate this kind of flora and fauna with Spain. But the Terre de l'Ebre biosphere reserve, located on the coast of southeastern Catalonia, is one of the largest wetlands in the Mediterranean. "When we anchored in the Ebro Delta, we felt like we had landed in Jurassic Park," says sailor Kirsten Pastijn. Behind the more than half-mile (1 km) long sandbar, there are numerous anchoring possibilities, with a nature park awaiting you on land where you can go hiking, cycling, kayaking, or birdwatching. The Dutchwoman and the Spaniard Gonzalo de Velasco love the fact that their floating home provides them with the opportunity to immerse themselves in new worlds of nature and cultures time and again.

When the 31- and 29-year-olds set up their company—an international platform for photographers—in 2019, their lives became bogged down in a routine they knew wouldn't make them happy in the long run: get up, have breakfast, work in the home office, make dinner, sleep ... and then wake up the next day to do it all again. At the weekend, they always drove as far as possible into nature—the main thing was to escape the city. Then Gonzalo had the idea of running their business from a boat, to wake up to fresh views every day. He has known how to sail since he was a child. His girlfriend leaped at the idea, and within three months they had given up their apartment and life in Madrid. In 2020, they moved onto their first sailing boat, a Puma 32. A year later, in the Port of Ibiza, they fell in love with a Feeling 1090, which had been neglected by its previous owner for some time, and purchased the larger sailboat. The crew of two christened the approximately 36 ft (11 m) long yacht *La Holandesa II,* and since then the Mediterranean has been their home and the salt water their front yard. When they lived on land, they always had to book a hotel or accommodation or pack a tent at the weekend if they wanted to go on vacation. Now they travel in the most beautiful way they can imagine and always have their home with them.

Together with their dog, Tinto, they have already explored the Mediterranean coasts of Spain and France by boat and enjoyed longer stops on Ibiza, Formentera, and Elba. One of their highlights was the medieval city of Tarragona in Catalonia, Spain. Where the Romans once landed their wooden galleys two thousand years ago, Kirsten and Gonzalo moored their fiberglass boat in the harbor. The friendliness of the people delighted them, and the many UNESCO World Heritage-listed buildings in the Old Town, such as the old amphitheater and the circus, meant their camera had no time off.

When we anchored in the Ebro Delta, we felt like we had landed in Jurassic Park.

When Gonzalo first told Kirsten about his idea of living on a floating home, images of the Caribbean appeared in her mind's eye and she instantly dreamed of swimming in the sea every day, lying on deck in the sun, and experiencing the world's most beautiful landscapes up close. This dream came true and is now part of their everyday life. However, to reach their dream spots, they have had to navigate through storms, high swells, and various challenges on several occasions. One tricky situation they encountered in the Gulf of Lion on the French Mediterranean coast is deeply etched in their minds. Numerous harbor handbooks warn of the gulf, which is known for its storms and strong winds. After a relaxing day of sailing under a bright blue sky, they and their yacht unexpectedly got caught in one of the region's characteristic storms, caused by the notorious tramontane wind. Assailed by nasty gusts, they still managed to get the mainsail down, but the headsail, her genoa, got awkwardly tangled and could no longer be furled. The lines lashed around with full force until the sail tore. One port refused them entry due to safety concerns, but they eventually managed to recover the tattered headsail behind a sheltered cliff while running the motor. In that sailing region, they learned the painful lesson of taking the worst forecast as the standard and making preparations accordingly.

Boat-life has changed them both. "We settle for a lot less now than we used to, and we've become a lot more down to earth as a result," Gonzalo says. They no longer feel the need to buy new clothes every month, and spend most of their time in swimwear or the same basics. If there is no supermarket in a bay, they simply fish for their dinner. They are not sure where they will go next—maybe they will be lured by the possibility of exploring the Greek islands. What they do know for sure, though, is: "Never put off your dreams until tomorrow, but live them now—if you have the resources to do so." ◄

SAILOR'S NOTES: SAILING WITH A DOG An increasing number of people are choosing to sail with pets: dogs, cats, and even chickens are sailing around the world! For the past few months, Kirsten and Gonzalo have also been sharing the good as well as the tough times on board with a four-legged crew member. Tinto, the dog, moved onto the yacht as a three-month-old puppy. After just four days, the Labradoodle had become so accustomed to boat-life that he recognized *La Holandesa II* among dozens of boats in the harbor. He always wears a life vest while sailing and is also attached to a long leash. Most of the time, however, he can be found dozing in the cockpit. As a puppy, with the help of puppy pads, Kirsten and Gonzalo showed him where he was allowed to do his business on board, so that now even longer sailing stages are feasible with their dog. His owners now provide him with new areas to explore on an almost daily basis, and, when they launch the dinghy while anchored, Tinto's anticipation knows no bounds.

Kirsten, Gonzalo, and their dog, Tinto, are exploring the Mediterranean coasts of Spain, France (next spread, right page), and Italy, with longer stops on Ibiza, Formentera, and Elba (right page, bottom). The *La Holandesa II*, a Feeling 1090, in the harbor at Barcelona (right page, top).

On their way to an anchorage off the vibrant port city of La Spezia in Liguria, Italy (previous spread, left page, bottom right), they sailed past the fortress at Le Grazie (this page, left). The charming coastal city of Dénia in Spain (this page, right, and right page, bottom right). View of the lighthouse at Portofino, Italy (right page, top).

ITALIE
Port de Garavan

CHARTING A COURSE FOR CREATIVITY

A SAYING WELL KNOWN to sailors is "Plans are written in sand at low tide." When it comes to boats, plans often go awry, as the Swiss Coline Amos and her French boyfriend, Maxime Kalenitchenko, discovered when water seeped through the keel bolts of their 42 ft (13 m) yacht, their very first vessel, the day after they bought it. At the time, the photographer and sports manager had already given up their jobs and the lease on their apartment. They were intending to embark on their big adventure—sailing from the French Mediterranean coast to the Caribbean—in just a few weeks' time. The three months of repair work meant that their Atlantic crossing had to be postponed by a year, as they would miss their window for avoiding hurricane season. They made the most of this unexpected turn of events by using the time to get better acquainted with the Mediterranean and their yacht, now given a new lease of life.

Coline grew up in a family of keen sailors. The 33-year-old has loved tales of adventure on the high seas from a young age. Later, she became inspired by the feats of female sailors like surfer Liz Clark, who lived alone on her 40 ft (12 m) boat and sailed the Pacific (page 156). For his part, 30-year-old Maxime was a complete novice when it came to sailing, but it was he who suggested to Coline that they leave their old lives behind and make a new start on a floating home. Coline agreed, and Maxime enrolled on a sailing course lasting several months.

For eight months now, this crew of two has been traveling around the Mediterranean on their 1990-built Dufour 42, which they christened the *Kalmos*. Having departed from the French mainland, they sailed to Corsica and then onward to the Pontine and Aeolian Islands in Italy, before winding up in the Aegean Islands of Greece. They spent the late summer in Sardinia and Italy, then headed west to discover the countless bays of the Balearic Islands.

"The smaller the island, the better," says Coline. The Aeolian archipelago in the Tyrrhenian Sea north of Italy is one of their all-time happy places. The lush landscape has an abundance of cactus, laurel, and bougainvillea species that bloom in a riot of colors, and is dotted with tiny villages of whitewashed houses.

In the little restaurants, fish dishes and regional specialties like arancini (stuffed and deep-fried rice fritters) come served on traditionally painted ceramics. "Every island has its own vibe. The people are so warm and welcoming, and no anchorage is same as the last," says Coline. Within the space of just two weeks, the couple went hiking on Panarea, saw blood-red lava spilling from the volcanic island of Stromboli while sailing at night, and visited the fishing village of Pecorini a Mare on the island of Filicudi, where they saw more donkeys than cars. "There's so much color everywhere, and you can really feel the artistic energy," says Coline.

The Kalmos *is just like home, only on the water.*

Creativity is hugely important to this two-person crew. If they are not hiking or snorkeling, or Maxime is not trail running in the mountains around the bay where they are anchored, they love to unwind through art. One of the most important items on board their vessel is their sewing machine, which has produced bags made from an old spinnaker sail, the flag for the *Kalmos,* and a small collection of T-shirts with prints. They love getting creative with others, too, and have a constant stream of visitors. The *Kalmos* can accommodate four extra crew members in the salon and the spare berth. "It's amazing to be able to share part of our adventure and show friends our way of life," says Maxime. They also love going ashore for picnics, playing board games for hours in the cozy salon, and organizing impromptu parties on the beach. In the immediate future, they are hoping to host a karaoke night in a bay, projecting song lyrics onto their main sail and inviting any nearby boats to take part. A friend once wrote in the guestbook, "The *Kalmos* is just like home, only on the water." Another visitor booked himself onto a sailing course straight after his stay.

Their worst experience so far was off the Italian island of Ischia, where they had anchored in a bay. They woke in the middle of the night to a powerful storm thundering overhead. The anchors of nearby boats broke loose in winds of over 45 knots (50 mph/80 kph), vessels crashed into each other, and their moored dinghy capsized. Thankfully, their yacht's anchor held and they were just far enough away from the neighboring boats not to collide. Since then, they have watched the live radar and weather forecasts more closely and always gather their things up in the evening so that nothing can tumble overboard.

They are planning to make their long-planned voyage across the Atlantic to the Caribbean in winter—no doubt with a few friends on board. After that, who knows? "La vraie liberté," says Coline—this is what true freedom looks like. ◄

SAILOR'S NOTES: THE TOP THREE ANCHORAGES, AS CHOSEN BY THE CREW OF THE *KALMOS*

The Italian island of Capraia is part of the Tuscan archipelago and lies 15 nautical miles (17 mi/28 km) east of Cap Corse. At its southern end, the bay of Cala Rossa is surrounded by alternating white and red rockfaces. "We went hiking on this wild island," recalls Coline. "The views were incredible, and the scent of Mediterranean Helichrysum and macchia hung in the air." The couple's second-favorite spot is on the western coast of Corsica, which is hugely popular with snorkelers. When they visited, they had Ficaghjola beach on the west coast to themselves. On the small beach, five picturesque old fishermen's houses nestle against the crags. Their third insider tip is Palmarola, one of Italy's Pontine Islands. Boats can anchor at the foot of striking white cliffs. Look closely, and you will spot a little wooden hut built into the cliff face. "We had a barbecue there and dived in underwater caves," says Coline.

A solitary walk on the island of Capraia, part of Italy's Tuscan Archipelago, was one of the highlights of the *Kalmos* crew's journey around the Mediterranean (right page). The *Kalmos,* a Dufour 42, near the island of Porquerolles off the French Mediterranean coast (previous spread).

matisse pond
KALMOS

View of Stromboli volcano on the island of the same name at sunrise (left page). For four weeks, Coline and Maxime explored Elba in the Tuscan Archipelago in their sailboat (this page). The crew has embellished the 1990s interior of their boat with graphic cushions, art posters, pictures, and contemporary ceramics (previous spread, right page, top left).

ONE COUPLE'S QUEST FOR CULTURE AND KITESURFING

PICTURE A BAY of turquoise water, surrounded by rocks and caves, and simply made for cliff-jumping and snorkeling. Cicadas chirrup in the bushy olive trees, and a historic little town with a maze of narrow streets lies just a short dinghy ride away down the coast. For over two years now, this movie-worthy scene has been the front yard of Catalina Eyzaguirre Fontaine, 30, and Juan Ignacio Vender, 40, who are exploring the Mediterranean in their 14-year-old Beneteau 49. "Traveling by boat gives you a whole new perspective on places and coastlines," enthuses Catalina. Although plenty of charter boats and day tourists ply the waters of the Mediterranean, the couple can often find a quiet place to anchor. They especially enjoy the evening hours, once the motorboats and sunseekers drift away into the golden light, leaving the bays to them and a few other sailboats from all over the world.

These two Chileans have already been able to check off a lot of sights and countries of the Mediterranean on their long bucket list, having taken their vessel, the *Buganvilia,* along France's Côte d'Azur, spent two months exploring Sardinia's photogenic bays, and traveled around Italy and Croatia. They are currently touring the Saronic Islands and Cyclades of the Aegean Sea. Their favorite anchorage so far has been a bay on the island of Lastovo, on the southern Adriatic coast, which belongs to an archipelago of around 50 islands. There they cast anchor in a glittering sea and attached the stern of their yacht to land with two ropes. Completely sheltered from the wind, they were able to kick back in the cockpit and drink in the views of lush green Mediterranean forests.

Of all the places in their log, they also have particularly fond memories of Mallorca. Along with the atmosphere of the island, they loved the variety of options for boaters. This island in the Spanish Balearics boasts a wealth of exquisite bays, including one near the enchanting village of Deià, another at the capital, Palma, and others in remote spots amid untrammeled nature, with spectacular views of the Serra de Tramuntana mountain range—a hiker's paradise in northwest Mallorca.

While others might use the Mediterranean to get their first taste of sailing and only work up the courage to do an Atlantic crossing later, Catalina and Juan did it the other way around. Having dreamed of swapping their fast-paced lives for a simpler, more sustainable way of living in harmony with nature, they gave up their apartment in 2020 and moved into an oceangoing yacht from the Caribbean that they had found online. Just a few weeks later, the couple crossed the Atlantic in 13 days, sailing from Bermuda to the Azores. Unlike Juan, Catalina had little previous experience of sailing, and she raves about seeing an orca leap out of the glassy, deep blue water right beside their floating home in the middle of the Atlantic. When they finally made it to Portugal, they were rightfully proud of themselves. "Tackling that crossing together really empowered us," says Catalina.

If the weather held, they could go kitesurfing right from their yacht.

Both of them are passionate kitesurfers and love playing with their kite, board, and the forces of nature whenever they get the chance. Combining their hobby with sailing can be tricky, as good kitesurfing spots do not tend to be located close to anchorages protected from the wind. They have had their best kitesurfing around Prasonisi, a rocky, roughly 1.2 mi² (3 km²) peninsula connected to Rhodes by a sandbar, and at Porto Pollo on the northern coast of Sardinia. If the weather held, they could go kitesurfing right from their yacht.

Originally, the couple intended to live on their boat only for a year, but they are now into their third. "Society is constantly sending us the message that we need more and more in order to be happy," says Catalina. "Flashier cars, more sophisticated clothing, bigger houses, better jobs. Life at sea changed my perspective on all that. I actually need less in order to be content. Nature and the ocean give me exactly what I need."

Where will their bow point next? Looking to the future, the nature-loving couple would love to circumnavigate the globe in a sailboat with an electric motor, sailing first to French Polynesia and eventually to their homeland of Chile. ◄

BOAT FACTS The boat's name, *Buganvilia,* is Spanish for bougainvillea. This native South America plant was the favorite of Juan's father, who taught him how to sail. By happy coincidence, the couple later learned that the French admiral and writer Louis-Antoine de Bougainville (1729–1811), after whom the plant was named, was the first Frenchman to circumnavigate the world. Their 49 ft (15 m) boat was built in 2008 by French yacht and motorboat manufacturer Beneteau. In the middle of the Covid-19 pandemic, they found it for sale on an online portal for $265,000. After they purchased it, the *Buganvilia* underwent a few upgrades before the pair embarked on their Atlantic crossing a few weeks later. Catalina and Juan replaced the mainsail and genoa and bought a gennaker and storm jib. Other enhancements included a chartplotter, a 12 V refrigerator, new interior upholstery and fenders, and a new motor for the anchor winch.

The crew's Greek island-hopping trip from Antipaxos to Ithaca took them past the island of Lefkada (previous spread). Kitefoiling straight from the boat (right page, top left). View from an anchorage off a Greek island at sunset (next spread).

The *Buganvilia,* a Beneteau 49, in turquoise waters off the Greek island Polýaigos, with a rugged rocky coastline in the background (previous spread). Like many sailors, Catalina and Juan store fresh fruit in hanging nets (this page, right).

View from an anchorage across to the lunar landscape of Milos, one of the Cyclades Islands in the Aegean Sea (this page). A small fishing village on Milos (right page, top). Reading on deck off Tonnara di Scopello, Sicily (right page, bottom left).

MANY ROUTES LEAD INTO THE GREAT BLUE YONDER

From hitchhiking and chartering to renting or buying, there are all sorts of ways to experience the freedom of boat-life and find the vessel and lifestyle of your dreams.

FROM COZY HOUSEBOATS and narrowboats to self-built rafts and lifeboats converted into floating homes, the boat-life scene celebrates all manner of approaches. More and more people, especially digital nomads, are finding themselves drawn to the idea of life on water, whether for an extended break or as an entire life change. Curiosity, a thirst for adventure, and a craving for an alternative lifestyle lure solo sailors, sailing groups, and families out of their comfort zone.

Putting boat-life to the test

Nowadays, there are plenty of ways to give life on the water a try, whatever your budget and need for comfort. For some time now, Airbnb has offered alternative types of accommodation among its properties—tiny houses, treehouses, caravans ... and boats. You can stay for a few nights on a raft in Germany, a narrowboat in the U.K., or a yacht in the Caribbean, all of which remain moored at a dock.

Chartering offers another way of delving a bit deeper into boat-life and gaining experience in different maritime regions without actually buying a boat. You can even book a captain for an extra charge. For those with a bit more time, there is the option of taking a few weeks to get your boat license. Newly qualified, you can then skipper your own charter boat from place to place.

Aspiring sailors who love socializing may want to join an existing crew. Skippers, couples, and families are always looking for temporary crew members for longer legs or to transfer their boats between anchorages. You help with the sailing, cooking, repair work, photography, or childcare on board, and get to sail for free in return, or you can charter berths for a daily, weekly, or monthly fee.

Thrill seekers will find special adventure sailing trips geared toward outdoor enthusiasts and sportspeople. The demand for custom-designed, sustainable trips in small groups is constantly rising, with packages ranging from multiday diving trips in French Polynesia to ski-and-sail holidays in Norway and climb-and-sail trips in Greece. Such boats often have room for just four to eight people on board, so plenty of camaraderie is guaranteed. Prior experience of sailing is not expected for these trips, but you get the opportunity to watch the crew at work and experience boat-life up close. Increasingly, these sorts of trips are associated with marine conservation projects. Ocean Missions, for instance, regularly plies Icelandic waters on a two-master with a hybrid electric motor and a mixed crew. These commercial research trips are aimed at students and anyone interested in marine sciences. "We believe in responsible tourism where the priority is to understand and connect with nature from the fully respect and curiosity. We want our guests to fall in love with the oceans and the art of sailing in order to raise the voice and speak for our oceans," says Ocean Missions founder Belén García Ovide.

Hitchhiking across the Pond

Those who are eager to get out of their comfort zone can join the worldwide boat hitchhiking movement and hitch a ride from port to port with a succession of crews. Hitchhiking hotspots along what is called the "Barefoot Route" in German—a traditional route that takes sailors from Europe across the Atlantic to the Caribbean—include Las Palmas on Gran Canaria and São Vicente in the Cape Verde Islands off the west coast of Africa. Several hundred crews set off from here between November and March every year, and word has gotten around the hitchhiking community. Sisters Julia and Lisa Hermes from Germany hitchhiked around the world, including an Atlantic crossing from Cape Verde to the Caribbean, all with no previous sailing experience. They met the four-person crew (including ship's cat Tara) who hosted them at the port itself. Spending 21 days and covering 2,300 nautical miles (2,650 mi/4,260 km) in the cramped 110 ft^2 (10 m^2) quarters with the three strangers had its challenges, but it also brought some new insights. "More than anything else, hitchhiking across the Atlantic taught us how to trust—to trust in others and in our ability to cope with a completely new environment," recall the sisters.

Those in the market for a sailboat will need to decide whether they fancy exploring the world in a classic monohull (left page), a catamaran (this page), or a trimaran.

Decision time: choosing a boat

If your ambitions go beyond pottering around inland waterways or hopping along the coast in your floating home—instead, you want to explore the world—then a cruising sailboat is the obvious choice. This allows you to cover far greater distances than with a motor yacht. This type of vessel also makes sailing less expensive and more sustainable, as the wind powers you from continent to continent, rather than burning diesel. Electric-powered vessels are still in their infancy, while solar-electric or fuel cell-powered boats have only had a few isolated successes on the oceans.

The market for cruising sailboats is even more eclectic than for camper vans. Sailboats of all ages from unknown and renowned shipyards alike are sold online and offline from secondhand markets and ports around the world. In many cases, they have undergone custom conversions or been retrofitted above and below deck by previous owners as part of refits. Due to the rise in demand for certain models, cruising aficionados often travel to other countries to purchase their dream boat. It is not uncommon for budding boat-lifers to glimpse a discreet "for sale" sign in a porthole on a stroll through the harbor, and secure their first vessel then and there.

As with vans, it is worth drawing a distinction between vintage sailboats that have already logged tens of thousands of nautical miles with their previous owners and brand-new cruisers, fresh from the shipyard, equipped with state-of-the-art technology and the ultimate in comfort. The right boat for you will depend on how much time and money you can invest in it and what you require of your vessel. Seasoned craftspeople and those keen to take on a project can buy a boat for a few hundred or thousand dollars and undertake their own refit. At the other end of the scale, you could invest your entire life savings in a boat in the six- or seven-figure range. Most boat-lifers pay a five-figure sum—somewhere in the middle.

Just as when looking for a house or apartment, you should ask yourself certain questions once you have worked out your budget for buying the boat itself and any upgrading and monthly overheads. How much space and comfort do you want? How big is the crew, and how many berths do you require? Where will you be sailing? How minimal can or should you go with the sails? How important is speed? You will come across all manner of vessels: small boats for exploring local waterways; sturdy seaworthy plastic vessels built and equipped specifically for ocean crossings and long-term cruising; swift, streamlined, and lightweight carbon yachts for regattas; and heavy boats made of aluminum or steel, designed to carry adventurers into polar waters. We generally distinguish between two types of boats. First, there are the classic one- or two-masted monohull vessels. These are particularly prevalent on the sailing scene, especially the versions with a keel. Although they tilt to the side in strong winds, the ballast in the keel keeps them afloat, even in heavy storms. Second, there are the multihulls, such as two-hulled catamarans, or trimarans with three hulls. These have far less of a slant while sailing and rock much less at anchor. They can also be significantly faster than keel boats of the same size, because the lack of a keel means that they displace less water in order to move forward. Thanks to their low draft, they can sail in shallow waters, too. The area between the hulls often contains a large dine-in kitchen with 360-degree views of the sea. The downside is that multihulls are more liable to capsize on rough seas, as they do not have the capacity to right themselves. When compared with monohulls that offer comparable living space, they also tend to be more expensive to buy and maintain.

One floating home, a multitude of possibilities

Weekend sailors often opt for a 20 to 26 ft (6 to 8 m) boat containing a mini cabin without much headroom, while solo sailors and couples tend to prefer boats of 33 to 39 ft (10 to 12 m) for easy sailing "shorthanded"—with a small crew. Families living full-time on their boats usually opt for 40 to 50 ft (12 to 15 m) yachts with more than two berths on board—comparable to a 380 ft² (35 m²) apartment.

These days, the average length of a boat used to cross the Atlantic is around 39 ft (12 m), but there are vessels that buck the trend. Take U.S. sailor Hugo Vihlen, for example, who crossed the stormy North Atlantic in 1993 in a micro yacht, with a hull length of just 5 ft 4 in (1.62 m). He holds the world record to this day. Houses cannot be described as definitively right or wrong, and the same goes for boats. What is true, however, is that safety and comfort generally increase with size.

Having your own sailboat allows you to sail to ports all over the world—like this one in the colorful fishing village of Bleik, northern Norway.

Boat sharing: The alternative to ownership

For those who love messing about in boats but do not want to live on one all the time, it may be worth clubbing together with a group of fellow boating enthusiasts to make your boating dream come true. As well as being more sustainable, this approach also pays off financially, as you get to share the purchase and running costs. Working together on a boat is a bonding experience, not to mention embarking on sailing adventures large and small to sound out and then fix any weak points on the boat.

Some fearless types have even been known to move onto a boat without ever having sailed before. This book reports on some of the adventures that ensued.

FROM VAN-LIFE TO BOAT-LIFE

INCREASING NUMBERS of people without a boating background are opting for a life on the water. It made perfect sense for Luca Fröhlingsdorf, whose motto in life is "the best plan is no plan." The 22-year-old was first introduced to boat-life by friends. In the spring of 2021, while in Tenerife, he bought an emerald-green Pearson 35 from 1968 on a whim. A couple of friends gave him a crash course in sailing—a few hours of explaining the basics in a rented dinghy, some taster trips on their catamaran, and then voyages on Luca's new yacht, the *Kala*. Having learned the ropes, Luca began cramming for his sports boat license, the German requirement for sailing a boat over 15 hp on the seas.

A digital nomad, Luca has always embraced freedom and spontaneity. After leaving school, he traveled across Europe while living in his camper van, nicknamed Vandrew. He spent most of the winter months on the Canary Islands with other van-lifers, his surfboard, and his dog, Nico. Compared with van-life, he appreciates the fact that living on a boat gives him far more space. His Volkswagen Transporter T5 lacked a sink, running water, or much headroom. "And the best thing about my boat is that it's a unique chance to live right on the water," he says, "instead of vaguely nearby."

He made his first long crossing from Tenerife to Fuerteventura via Gran Canaria, with three friends aboard. While out at sea near Fuerteventura, his engine failed twice in a short space of time, so he had to be towed back to port. While his vessel was undergoing repairs, Luca got to know Claudius Brünn, the sailor moored next to him. They often go sailing together, and in summer 2022 Claudius was Luca's co-captain on a voyage from the Canaries to the Mediterranean. Luca had long been dreaming of traveling to the Mediterranean to escape the poor protection offered by anchorages in the Canaries and the Atlantic swell, which made the *Kala* rock too much for comfort. He was also longing to experience the wonders of the Mediterranean from his new home, hear the strains of great music on the warm breeze, and gaze out over calm, crystal-clear seas.

After a two-week stop at the marina in Agadir on the Moroccan coast, he and Claudius sailed through the

Strait of Gibraltar and into the Mediterranean. Almost immediately, they were greeted by a passing thunderstorm. "When I looked out and saw lightning in the distance, I did wonder just what on earth would happen to us and the boat if the storm got any closer," he says. "That was when I realized that, for all that I had learned about sailing, fundamentally I still knew next to nothing."

So far, the Spanish Balearics top Luca's list of favorite Mediterranean regions. He is especially keen on Ibiza because of its laidback atmosphere. Arriving in Ibiza for the first time in his yacht was a truly magical moment—he recalls sailing between the island and the sacred rock of Es Vedrà with a gentle wind behind the sails in a butterfly position. When in Ibiza, he likes to anchor at Cala d'Hort or Cala Comte on the western side of the island. From Cala Comte, he can then paddle his dinghy to the Sunset Ashram Beach Bar and listen to chill-out DJ sounds as the sun sets in a blaze of color behind the bay. His boat is currently at a harbor on the French island of Corsica, waiting for its next adventure with this novice sailor.

When I looked out that night and saw the lightning, I did wonder what on earth would happen to us.

Luca does not live on his 36 ft (11 m) home full-time, but heads straight there when his craving for sea air and that unrivaled sense of freedom becomes too strong to ignore. In between, he usually spends several weeks a year with his family in Germany. The rest of the time is devoted to his work as a talented portrait and fashion photographer, for which his travels have taken him to Copenhagen, Paris, and New York City.

Luca, who sports a mop of blond hair, is not planning to sail around the world, but he is eager to venture farther into the Mediterranean, explore the bays around Corsica and Sardinia, and spend the summer months island-hopping in Greece. But nothing is set in stone, of course.

"My boat has taught me to be patient, persevere, and not let others deter me from living out my dreams," says Luca. Those who know him have occasionally accused him of naivete or a lack of sense, but he believed in his dream, fought for it, and made it happen. He advises budding boat-lifers to go sailing with their friends as much as possible, or to take part in sailing trips. "I wish everyone could feel the freedom that I do," he says, his eyes shining. "Sitting right at the front, in the pulpit, gazing out to the horizon and hearing the boat moving through the waves is the best feeling ever."

BOAT FACTS Lucas's *Kala,* a Pearson 35, was built in the late 1960s. U.S.-based Pearson Yachts was one of the first manufacturers to build fiberglass sailboats. The yacht, which is bursting with retro appeal and is seen as the waterborne counterpart to the iconic Volkswagen Bus, has a double berth at the bow, a bathroom, and a salon with a galley kitchen and seating area. The German sailor paid the previous owner on Tenerife around €18,000 ($19,000) for the solid boat with its canting keel, cozy interior, and spacious cockpit. Luca later installed an autopilot system, fitted solar cells, and invested in a new dinghy with an outboard motor. He has also made some interior upgrades, including sprucing up the bathroom and a new galley kitchen, replacing the curtains, and creating a cozy atmosphere with cushions, blankets, and plants.

From the Canary Islands, Luca sailed through the Strait of Gibraltar and into the Mediterranean Sea. On the way, he made a two-week stop in the coastal city of Agadir and explored the coast of Imsouane, where he took lots of photographs (previous spread, left page, and next spread, top left and bottom).

CUISINE

The emerald-green *Kala,* a Pearson 35, off the coast of Tenerife in the Canary Islands, where Lucas's boat-life began (this page). A sailboat off the sacred rock of Es Vedrà, southwest of Ibiza in the Balearic Islands, where Luca experienced a magical moment in his boat (right page).

Ohana

TAKING THE SLOW ROUTE TO HAWAII BY CATAMARAN

ELENA DOSTAL and Ben Schaschek's catamaran is called Ohana—"family" in Hawaiian. The German couple are gradually gearing up to sail to the island state. They have been living on a boat ever since 2019—first on a 30 ft (9 m) monohull and, since summer 2020, on their 38 ft (11.5 m) long and 21 ft (6.5 m) wide catamaran, which offers far more space and comfort.

Independently of one another, Elena, 29, and Ben, 36, both decided that the well-trodden path through life was not for them. They could not imagine working nine to five and always longed to go traveling and see the world. "A boat is perfect for that, as you can take your home with you the whole time," says Elena. They move on to a new country every couple of months. For the first two years, the trained foreign-language correspondent and sound engineer made their living by taking people on sailing trips. Today, they focus on their social media channels and their online shop, which sells handmade ceramics from Portugal.

Their catamaran, a Lagoon 380 S2 built in 2008, was once a classic charter boat. They bought it in Croatia for €130,000 ($138,000) and converted it to suit their needs, with loving attention to detail. This involved transforming a functional-looking seating nook into a corner sofa and installing a new galley kitchen, complete with a dishwasher and a cozy wood-burning stove. They painted the walls and decorated them with lots of bohemian details in shades of sand and cream. The four berths are now a sleeping cabin, a laundry with a washing machine, a tool room, and a space for the couple's beloved surfboards and other paraphernalia. The *Ohana* got a new look on the outside, too: an artist friend worked with them to create a large-scale dreamcatcher image and spray-painted it onto the hull.

Elena and Ben took their vessel to Portugal first, having previously been awed by its rocky coastline. Their favorite spot on the Algarve, on Portugal's southern coast, is Alvor, which lies between Lagos and Portimão. There they anchored in a lagoon alongside a charming little fishing village. Dinner was easy: clams for fresh *spaghetti alle vongole* were just a stone's throw away. The photogenic bays of the Balearics and Sardinia are much-loved haunts. "Sardinia's coastline is incredibly varied," says Elena. "In midsummer, though, both places are swarming with tourists, so it's better to go when things are quieter." They are particularly fond of Formentera, the smallest island in the Balearics. "The water is clearer and bluer than in the Caribbean, and the sand is as soft as in Australia's Whitsunday Islands," says Ben. As far as these two are concerned, the only downside is the lack of surfable waves. But they love the warmth of the locals, the traditional food made with fresh produce, and the fact that the next island is just a day or two's sailing away.

Being close to land is important to Elena and Ben, as they work from the *Ohana* and need to be able to travel without being offline for weeks on end. As their vessel is fitted with solar cells, a watermaker, and a boiler, they are fairly self-sufficient, so they only bother with fee-charging harbor spots on rare occasions. Their floating office does, however, depend on well-protected anchorages. When traveling around the Canaries, they found working on board difficult at times, as the boat was rocked so violently by the wind and waves. Besides working on their laptops, boat repairs are high on their daily to-do list. "Anyone who's ever lived or traveled on a boat will know that there's always something to fix from one bay to the next," says Elena. "There's always something going wrong on a boat."

The water is clearer and bluer here than in the Caribbean.

During their time in the Mediterranean, they have met many retired folk living full-time on their monohulls and multihulls. But they are being joined by increasing numbers of people their own age. So where next for these two free spirits? They both stand by the dictum "When you sail, never stick to a plan." Ben, who spent four years sailing around the world with a friend when he was younger, would have preferred to stay in the Mediterranean for another year, but Elena was eager to set off for the Caribbean straightaway. They agreed on a compromise: they would start by sailing to the Azores, then onward to Madeira and the Cape Verde Islands in the Atlantic. Right now, Hawaii is some 10,000 miles (16,000 km) away as the crow flies. "It will take another five to six months even if we were to sail straight through. But there are so many countries along the way that we don't want to miss," says Elena. So much is there to see that they reckon they will only be saying "Aloha" to their families and followers from Hawaii five or even ten years from now.

SAILOR'S NOTES: ANCHORAGES IN FORMENTERA The anchorage of Es Pujols is located right next to the idyllic holiday resort of the same name. Elena and Ben like to visit the stalls on the beach, which sell homemade local wares. They can moor their dinghy at the jetty itself. "It's best to moor the boat at sunset, soak up the Spanish vibes, and just feel yourself drifting," says Elena. The couple are also big fans of the bays on either side of the Platja de Ses Illetes. You can anchor in crystal-clear water 6½ to 13 ft (2 to 4 m) deep, with white sand beaches and postcard-perfect, Caribbeanesque views. Besides making the most of the sweeping beach, the couple recommend the 40-minute walk along the sand to the town's picturesque harbor.

Elena and Ben, the musical crew of the *Ohana* (right page, top right), have so far traveled to Portugal, the Canary Islands, and the Mediterranean in their eye-catching catamaran, a Lagoon 380 S2 (right page, bottom).

Elena's favorite spot on deck is the outsize hammock swinging in the cockpit (left page). The couple has transformed their functional charter catamaran into a floating home by painting the walls, laying new floors, and giving the galley kitchen a bright upgrade (this page, right). They like to decorate with natural materials in pale shades (previous spread, top left, and this page, left).

BETWEEN BUTTERFLIES AND SOUL FOOD IN THE TURKISH AEGEAN

A BOAT IS MOORED in front of bright green pinewood slopes that are reflected in the crystal clear, pool-like water; colorful schools of fish, sea turtles, and squid swim under the keel, and between the bushes roam not only sheep and goats, but the occasional fox or porcupine, too. This backdrop has an acoustic accompaniment provided by owls with their call reverberating through the night in the light of the full moon. "Turkey feels like the oasis of the Mediterranean," enthuses 34-year-old sailor Kristina Avdeeva. Together with her 33-year-old boyfriend, Niko Tsarev, she prefers to sail along Turkey's rugged Aegean coast in the low season between October and April, when there are only a few boats out and about, enjoying the numerous secluded anchorages and peninsulas.

Eight years ago, Kristina, who traveled a lot in her private and professional life, was looking for a new hobby and obtained a sailing license. A short time later, she met Niko and infected the motorboat pilot with her enthusiasm for sailing. Since then, the creative couple—Kristina is a photographer, director, and writer, and Niko is a director of photography and producer—has been traveling every year for several months on a chartered sailboat. However, the two rarely sail alone. Under the name *Sea Soul,* emblazoned as a minimalist logo on their red flag, they share their travels with friends, acquaintances, and people who follow them on Instagram, to share both the charter boat expenses and their experiences. They want their guests to feel like part of the maritime community. "We are crazy, altruistic people who are happy to open up the world of sailing to others," Kristina says.

While they were still living in Saint Petersburg and Moscow, they constantly had the desire to escape to the wilderness to breathe freely. For them, boat-life represents autonomy and independence. They describe their adventure as "slow sailing" and do not aspire to circumnavigate the globe in the near future. Sitting in the cockpit at night under millions of stars and listening to the sound of the waves, they find it easy to reflect on their own lives and ponder the universe. "When you don't have floods of news raining down on you every day and you're cut off from social media, you regain a sense for real life and your true self again," Kristina muses.

The freedom lovers had previously chartered sailboats to sail between the Lipari Islands of Italy, in Croatia, in Greece, and in the Seychelles, but no place has caught their imagination as much as the southern coast of Turkey. They have been sailing in the Turkish Aegean for several years now. Right now, they are spending an entire year in their favorite place. This corner of the planet is for them one of the most beautiful and comfortable sailing regions they know. They like the warm climate, the top-quality service in the ports, the moderate wind, the hospitality of the locals, and the culinary variety. "Turkish cuisine—just like the people here—is very diverse. I get the same feeling here like I did when I was on summer vacation with my grandma," Kristina says.

In spring, the blooming coastal landscape of the Aegean replicates the floral pattern of a carpet.

One of their favorite sailing spots is the area around the idyllic Gemiler Island, also called St. Nicholas Island, where you can anchor in bays or moor with shorelines. The small island, where the original tomb of St. Nicholas of Myra is said to have been located, is famous for its ancient church ruins. A little farther east along the mainland coast, you have the option of anchoring in Butterfly Valley cove. In the valley behind the gorge-like cove with a white sandy beach, which can be reached only by boat, cliff faces rise up to 1,148 ft (350 m). Numerous colorful butterfly species live there, giving the cove its name. Also located nearby is the giant Babadağ, a mountain some 6,560 ft (2,000 m) high, which is ideal for hiking and paragliding. The Russian crew likes spring best, when the wildflowers and trees awaken and the blooming coastal landscape replicates the floral pattern of a Turkish carpet. But even in winter, they're still known to leap into the crystal-clear sea at a water temperature of 72°F (22°C), and in the coldest month of January they have never experienced days with an outside temperature of lower than 60°F (15°C).

This year, Kristina and Niko took a big step toward full-time boating life: they moved from Russia to Turkey and now live in a small house just a two-minute walk from a marina. There, they either help out other sailors or charter their favorite boat, a Dufour 470 with bunks for eight below deck. "Every day, we gain new experiences here and are preparing for our big dream of buying our own sailboat soon," says Niko. ◄

SAILOR'S NOTES: THE CREW'S TOP THREE DESTINATIONS ON THE TURKISH AEGEAN

The micro area of the Gulf of Göcek, which has a diameter of about 10 nautical miles (11.5 mi/19 km), is one of Kristina and Niko's favorite spots. Here, you can find more than two dozen small and well-protected anchorages surrounded by beautiful nature. In some of the bays, there are restaurants only accessible to boat owners. Those who dine here are usually allowed to moor at the adjoining moorings or jetties free of charge. The crew's favorite restaurant bays include Adaia, Kapi Creek, and Tomb Bay. Ayvalık is their favorite Turkish town. They like the unique atmosphere and architecture of the port town located on the Aegean coast opposite the Greek island of Lesbos. In the off-season, they particularly like to head for an unnamed cove opposite Soğuk Su Koyu. The bay, which is almost completely enclosed by sheer cliffs, has room for just one or two boats, and there is a small sandy beach just around the corner.

Kristina and Niko's chartered boat moored at the Karacaören Restaurant in the Turkish Aegean (previous spread). View of the lighthouse on the Datça Peninsula (right page). Fishermen offshore from the city of Kuşadası (next spread, left page). Turkish specialties served in the cockpit (next spread, right page, top). The Greek island of Tilos (next spread, right page, bottom left).

HIRÇIN DENIZ

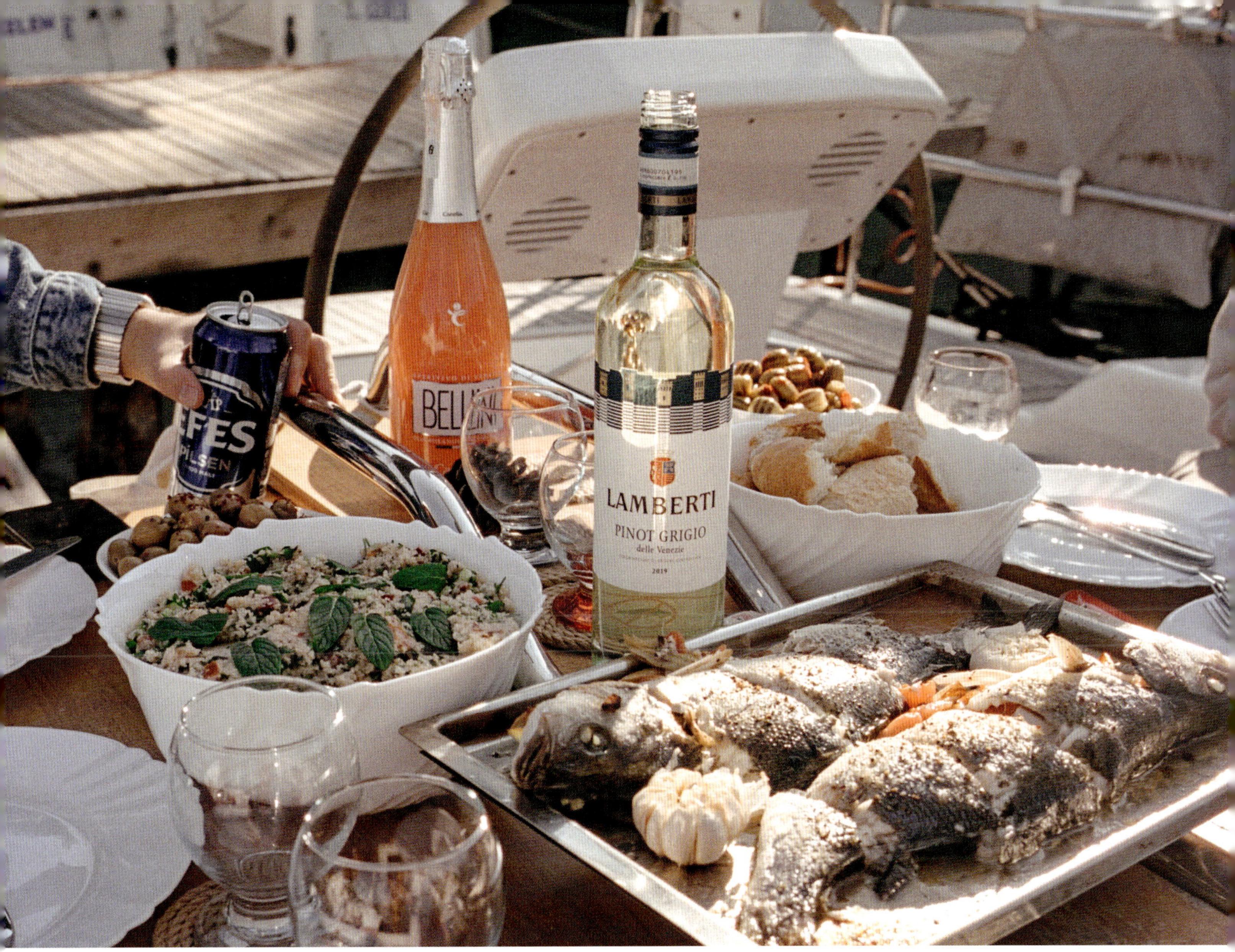
EFES
PILSEN
BELLINI
LAMBERTI
PINOT GRIGIO
delle Venezie
2019

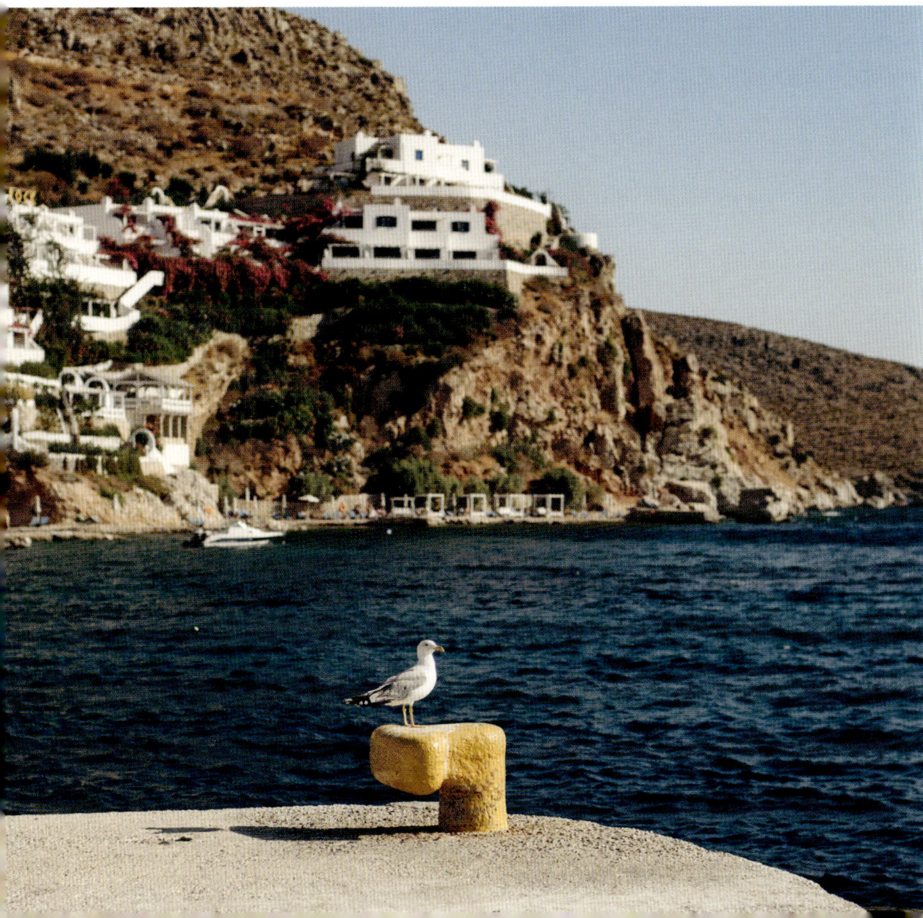

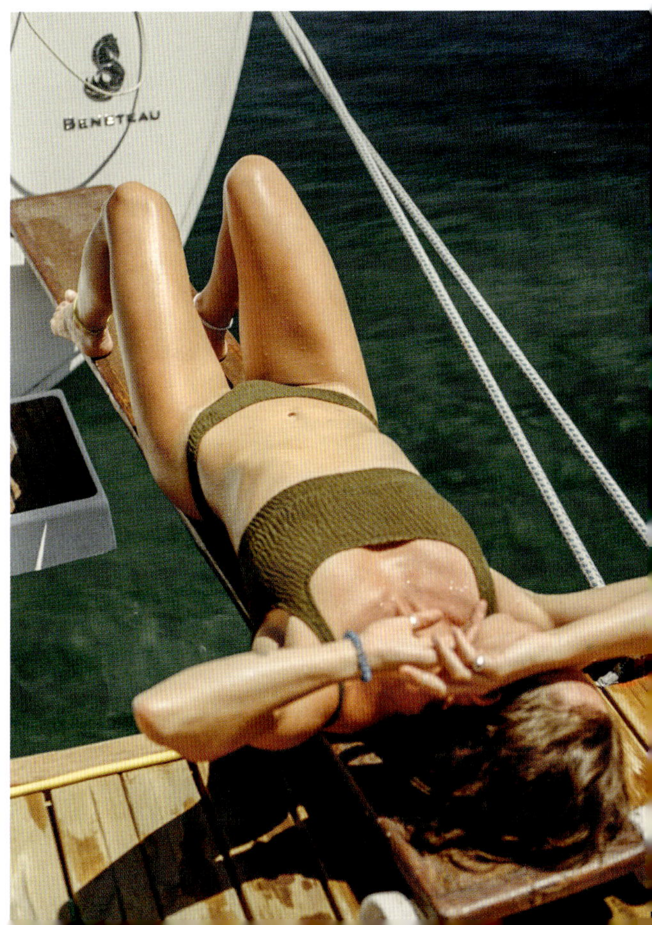

BENETEAU

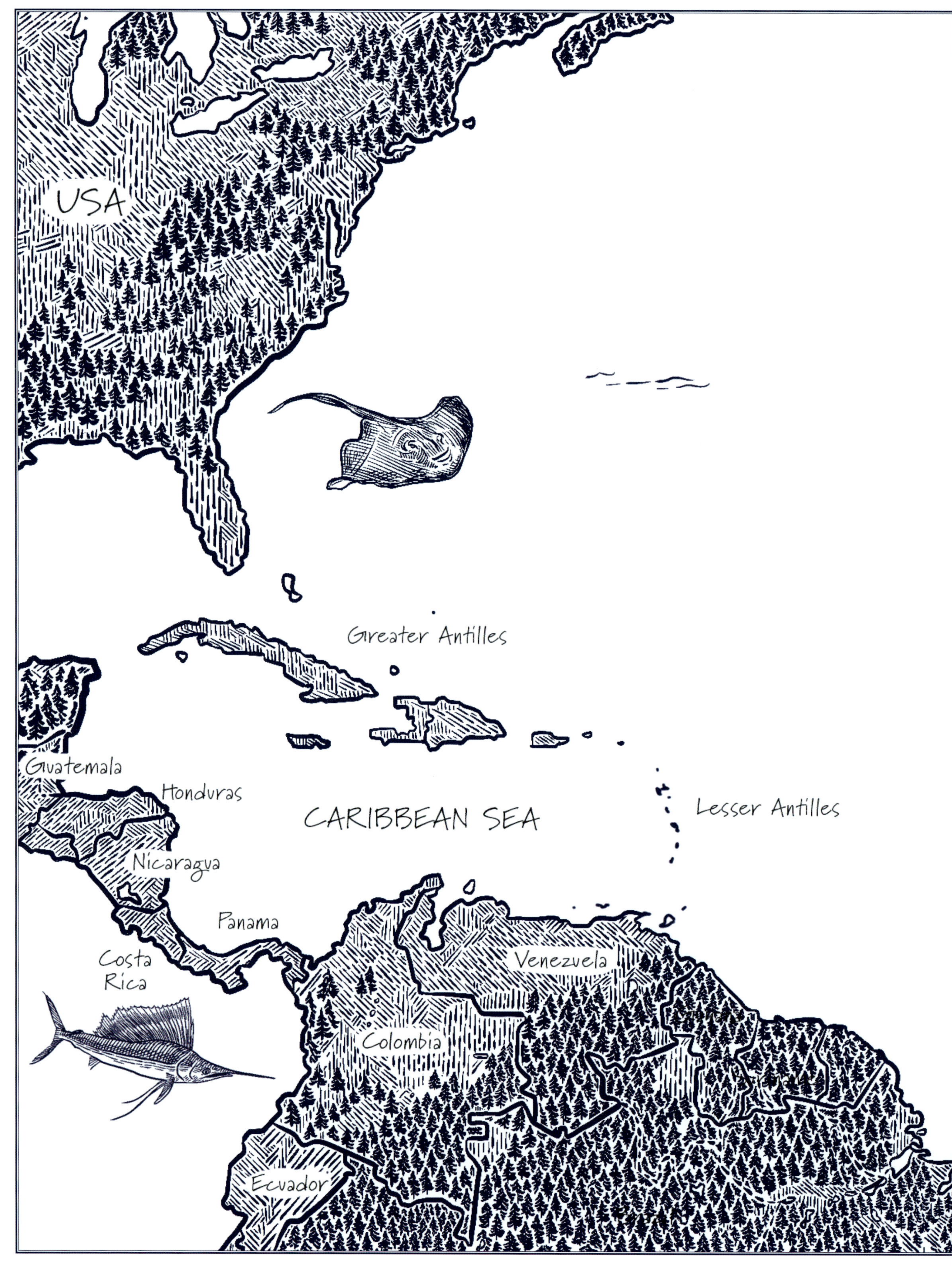
USA
Greater Antilles
Guatemala
Honduras
CARIBBEAN SEA
Lesser Antilles
Nicaragua
Panama
Costa
Rica
Venezuela
Colombia
Ecuador

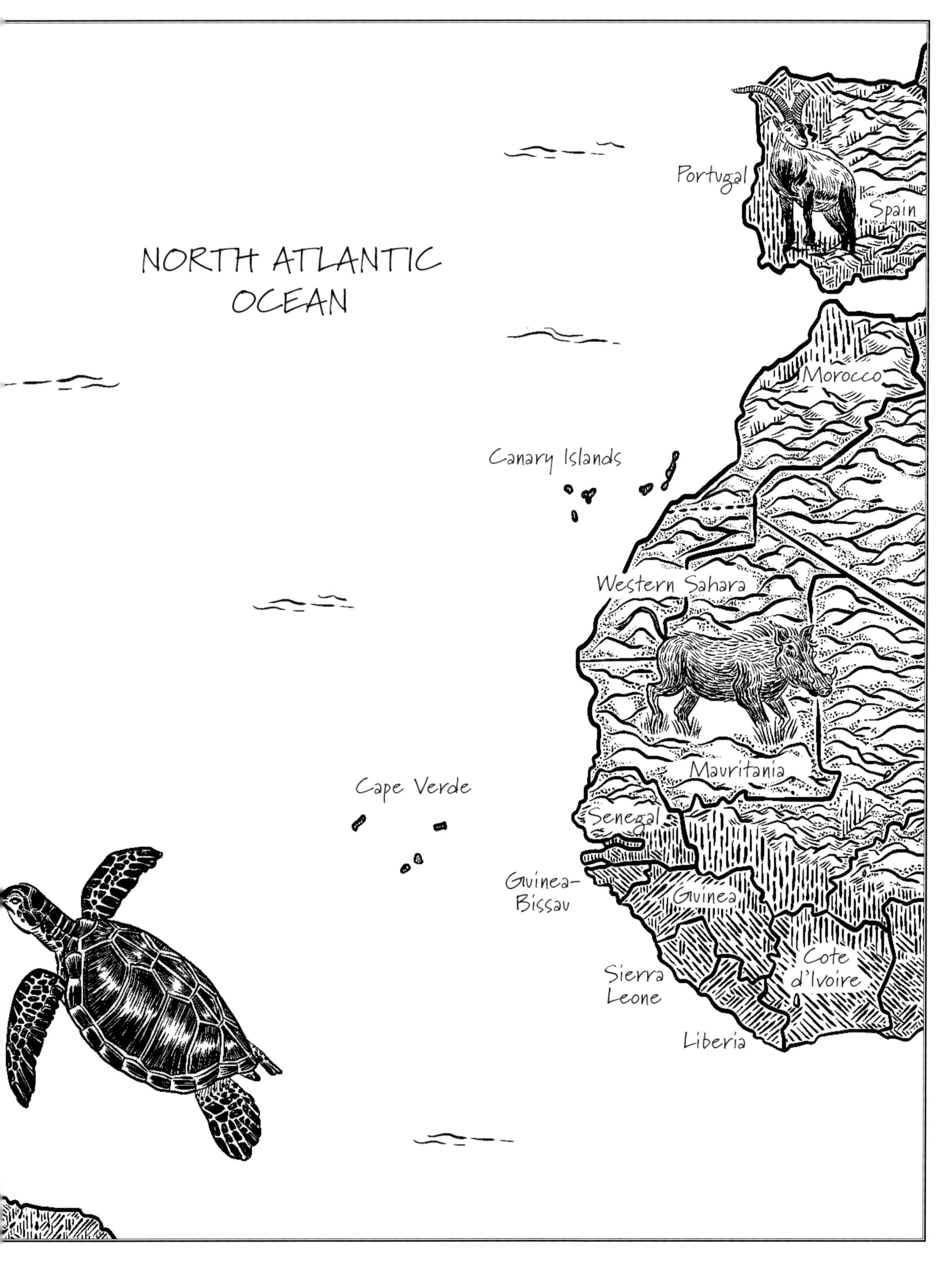
NORTH ATLANTIC
OCEAN
Portugal
Spain
Morocco
Canary Islands
Western Sahara
Mauritania
Cape Verde
Senegal
Guinea-
Bissau
Guinea
Sierra
Leone
Liberia
Cote
d'Ivoire

FROM SWEDEN TO THE CARIBBEAN AND BACK AS A MATURE GAP YEAR

TAKING A YEAR of unpaid leave, Swedish couple Hedvig von Essen and Mattias Wernersson fulfilled the dream of many a permanent employee and embarked on an unforgettable adventure. The two bought a boat and sailed across the Atlantic to the Caribbean and back to Stockholm in 12 months. They did not have much sailing experience, so they initially invested in a small Scampi 30 and together learned to tack and jibe on the Baltic Sea. A year later, they bought their Hanse 411, a 17-year-old, 41 ft (12 m) performance cruiser, and took up their nomadic life.

The then 28- and 30-year-olds sailed the *Monkii* through the English Channel, navigated the Bay of Biscay from Roscoff in France to San Sebastián on the northern Spanish coast, and reached the Canary Islands after barely three months. They had a fixed start date in their diaries for their Atlantic crossing from Gran Canaria because they had signed up for the Atlantic Rally for Cruisers (ARC). The ARC is an annual competition for which sailing and regatta crews can register under certain conditions and for an entry fee. Since neither had much sailing experience, it was a good opportunity for them to race the leg surrounded by 140 other yachts.

"At the start of our Atlantic crossing, I was counting every nautical mile and minute. But once a few days have passed and there is no land in sight, you reach a state of Zen in the middle of the ocean, where you learn to appreciate the beauty of nature, marine life, and sailing," Hedvig says. But even that Zen state can get out of kilter from time to time. "It did feel like a roller-coaster ride at times. Your emotional state is extremely dependent on the weather, and your mood reflects that," Mattias says. The first crossing was quite rough with wind speeds of 30 knots (40 mph/56 kph) at times, 13 to 16 ft (4 to 5 m) waves, and heavy squalls and rain showers, which made it difficult for the crew to live a relaxed life on board. In addition, Hedvig and Mattias's autopilot refused to work, so they had to steer the entire leg by themselves. They got help from four friends, with whom they took turns steering and trimming the sails every three hours.

One of the horror scenarios that every sailor dreads occurred on day eight: their watermaker stopped when they were down to 1.6 gal (6 L) of drinking water, a few sodas, and some milk on board. Two days later, they finally found the fault, thus allowing them to feel more relaxed about the remaining nautical miles. After 18 energy-sapping days, they finally arrived in St. Lucia in the Caribbean.

In contrast, their return journey was considerably smoother, contrary to all sailing wisdom about the North Atlantic's ever-changing moods. They sailed the longest leg between Bermuda and the Azores in 14 days with just the two of them—a working autopilot, consistent weather, and their greater experience made a major difference. Listening to podcasts, reading, letting thoughts meander, and gazing at the sea for hours became everyday life for Hedvig and Mattias. Dolphin spotting and digital detox were part of their daily itinerary, and any tension only had to be dealt with between themselves and not among a crew of six. One of their favorite moments was an outdoor movie night using their mainsail as the projection screen, complete with homemade popcorn. Their best investment was the impromptu purchase of a barbecue. "Cooking the fish we caught ourselves in the Atlantic right on board was a truly unique experience," Hedvig recalls.

Once a few days have passed and there's no more land in sight, you get into a state of Zen in the middle of the ocean.

They had five months between their Atlantic crossings to experience the Caribbean's multifaceted nature. Their route took them along the eastern Caribbean islands, which are often only a day's sailing apart. From St. Lucia, they crossed to St. Vincent and the Grenadines. From there, they continued northward via Martinique, Guadeloupe, and St. Martin to the Turks and Caicos Islands as well as the Bahamas and Bermuda, from where they commenced their journey home.

Every four to seven days they changed anchorage in the Caribbean Sea, which they usually shared with several dozen sailboats that also drifted along this standard route. Crooked Island in the Bahamas was their favorite port of call. With a population of around 300 people, the island sits in a shallow lagoon. Hedvig and Mattias anchored in a secluded bay and stopped at Gibson's Restaurant. Here they experienced the owner's hospitality and phenomenal cooking skills. The next day, her sons invited them on an underwater adventure, diving with them to collect shells, spear fish, and feed sharks.

So, would they cross the Atlantic again? Most definitely! But first, they want to set a course north, as Norway beckons. ◀

SAILOR'S NOTES: THE *MONKII'S* CREW THREE FAVORITE PLACES IN THE CARIBBEAN Hedvig and Mattias have many special memories of their engagement on Green Island, a small uninhabited island off the Atlantic east coast of the Caribbean island of Antigua, as well as of the many paradisiacal anchorages. They spent hours snorkeling the surrounding reefs, which are home to rays, turtles, and numerous starfish. The island of Terre-de-Haut is part of Guadeloupe and is known for its stunning beaches. The Swedish couple also hiked here to the green peak of Morne du Chameau, which is some 1,000 ft (300 m) high. Anchoring in the crystal-clear waters off Mayaguana, the easternmost island of the Bahamas, is also in their top three. For about two nautical miles (2.3 mi/3.7 km), the crew had to carefully navigate along reefs to get to their anchorage, which resembled a scene on a postcard. "The water was so shallow and clear there that you could watch marine life from the deck," Hedvig enthuses.

A hike to Mount Pelée, the highest volcano in Martinique (right page, bottom). The *Monkii,* a Hanse 411, at anchor in the turquoise waters of the Bahamas (next spread, left page, top). Hedvig on the Caledonian Canal in Scotland (next spread, right page). Grilling fish caught by the crew in the Caribbean (next spread, left page, bottom left).

STEERING A COURSE BETWEEN RAYS AND REMOTE WORKING

BOASTING CORAL GARDENS, deep-sea canyons, wrecks lying 130 ft (40 m) below the surface, and water teeming with turtles, stingrays, octopuses, and parrotfish, it is no wonder that Guadeloupe and its underwater realm were so admired by diving pioneer and marine scientist Jacques-Yves Cousteau that it become one of his favorite bases back in the 1950s. Around 70 years later, oceangoing nomads Alexandra Lakin and Lars Sandved Smith in turn discovered the Jacques Cousteau Underwater Reserve on the western side of the island, a haven for diving, snorkeling, and free diving. In January 2022, they crossed the Atlantic in 17 days, sailing from the Cape Verde Islands in their yacht, *Navika,* and have been exploring the tropics in the 1981-built Tayana 37 ever since. They will never forget the moment they glimpsed land on the horizon again after their ocean crossing. "It was so thrilling to arrive somewhere completely new in our floating home. That's probably what makes ocean sailing so addictive," says Alexandra.

When Alexandra, from France, and Lars, from Sweden, first met many years back, they found that they shared the dream of swapping their busy city life for boat-life. Both of them had the right sort of experience under their belts: as a teenager, Alexandra used to sail among the islands of Brittany, while Lars had boated around the Swedish archipelagos. Four years ago, at the age of 30, they realized that they had been treading water and waiting for the perfect moment to come along, but that there would never be a time when everything fell exactly into place. In that newfound clarity, they both quit their permanent jobs without knowing what lay ahead. Online searches turned up a boat in Spain for €50,000 ($60,000), which they promptly bought.

But before they could cast off, their 37 ft (11 m) boat required a major upgrade to transform it from a weekend pleasure boat into an oceangoing vessel. While living on board in a harbor in the south of France, they installed a wind generator, solar panels, a hot-water boiler, watermaker, new navigation equipment, a radar system, and an AIS radio system, and also replaced the anchor. They laboriously restored the teak deck and invested in a fixed dinghy with a large outboard motor. Six months later, the two-person crew finally left port and spent a year and a half in the Mediterranean, sailing around Corsica, Sardinia, and the Balearics, and getting to know the coast of mainland Spain. Then came the Atlantic and the Caribbean. Besides Guadeloupe, Dominica in the eastern Caribbean also cast its spell on them. It more than lived up to its nickname of "Nature Island," and they ended up staying a whole two months. The couple visited waterfalls, mountains, the rainforest, and thermal springs on this pristine island, which has not yet been overrun by mass tourism. "Everyone knows everyone here, so we were able to immerse ourselves in local life and get to know people really quickly," recalls Alexandra. They found lots of like-minded souls among the Caribbean sailing community, too—lots of people here live on their sailboats, while charter boats and coast-hoppers are few and far between.

Dominica more than lived up to its nickname of "Nature Island." It cast its spell over the crew for a whole two months.

Having crossed the Atlantic, Alexandra and Lars decided to slow down a little. They are eager to settle into local communities a bit more, get active, and anchor alongside friendly fellow sailors. No two days are the same. After their morning routine of swimming, yoga, and coffee on deck, they might do some boat maintenance, go hiking, do a few laps on their stand-up paddleboard, or dive beneath the waves. They have been working remotely from their boat for some time. Lars is completing his PhD, while Alexandra captures their lifestyle for her YouTube channel. They also run an online meditation platform together. Of course, when they need to work, they have far less time for exploring or going on mini adventures. Searching for cellular reception can be challenging and means that they are more likely to linger in places. Both of them are still getting used to this aspect of their new life.

Alexandra and Lars found this remote anchorage with an imposing rocky backdrop off the Mediterranean island of Mallorca and spontaneously decided to stop there for the night (previous spread). Sardinia ahoy (right page, top). Yoga on deck or ashore is an indispensable part of Alexandra's daily routine in the Caribbean (right page, bottom left).

For the crew of the *Navika,* boat-life comes with plenty of magical highs, but there are occasional lows, too. The rough-and-ready nature of things has challenged the couple in ways that they never expected. "In the past, we often made the mistake of comparing life on board to our previous life, which made it even more difficult to deal with any problems or inconveniences," says Alexandra. Adopting a more flexible mindset has helped them to adapt to living within a confined space, turbulent anchorages, and sudden storms at sea, and to get through them together. "If you want to live on a boat, you have to be OK with the fact that something unforeseeable can happen at any moment. You have to be prepared to cast any preconceived ideas aside," she says.

SAILOR'S NOTES: FREE DIVING FROM THE BOAT

In Dominica, Alexandra and Lars took consecutive free-diving courses at a diving school. This taught them the basics of free diving safely, so that they could start diving from their boat, securely tethered to a line. At a certain depth, the human body begins to sink on its own—a feeling that Alexandra describes as "flying in slow motion." She can now free-dive 130 ft (41 m) deep, while Lars can reach a whopping 207 ft (63 m). They are captivated by the silence underwater—free diving is undisturbed by bubbles or diving regulators. In the Caribbean, the couple could even hear the whales. With their newly acquired diving skills, they can explore the underwater kingdom around their anchorages without excessive equipment: all they need is their free-diving masks, which have a lower inbuilt volume of air than standard masks; snorkels; fins; and hooded wetsuits and weight belts. They also use a free-diving buoy so that they can be seen by other boats.

Navika

The *Navika* at anchor on the northern side of the Balearic island of Mallorca (this page). A happy crew: Alexandra and Lars at anchor on their Tayana 37 sailboat (right page). The crew was escorted by dolphins for part of their Atlantic crossing to the Caribbean (next spread, left page). In Dominica in the Lesser Antilles, the couple learned to free dive from a platform (next spread, right page).

NORTH ATLANTIC OCEAN, CARIBBEAN SEA
& MEDITERRANEAN SEA

ZIGZAGGING THEIR WAY FROM THE U.K. TO GUADELOUPE

JESSICA SCHOELLER-SZÜTS and Jan-Hendryk Büse could not believe their eyes when they crossed from the Canary Island of Tenerife to Cape Verde in the middle of December in just under six days: it suddenly started to rain shooting stars from the sky one of the nights. Only later did they discover that they had witnessed one of the most intense meteor showers of the year, the Geminids.

This moment was just one of many that confirmed to the Austrian and the German that they had chosen the right path in life two years earlier. The desire to live differently had been the impetus for the 36- and 37-year-olds to change the course of their lives that had been comfortable until that moment. Boat-life, van-life, or emigrate to Australia? There were options aplenty for the two self-employed professionals, as they could work from anywhere. "We felt increasingly disconnected from urban life and our work routine at the time. We wanted to live with less and experience more," Jessica says. Jan, who had spent his youth sailing dinghies, had long dreamed of eventually buying and sailing a boat around the world. Jessica had no sailing experience, but as a passionate traveler and amateur diver, she quickly embraced the idea of living and working at sea. Within a few months, they had given up their apartment, sold their furniture and cars, and invested in a spacious bluewater boat, a Contest 48CS.

They found the *Adhara* in the U.K. in 2020. From there, the interior designer and journalist and the entrepreneur first sailed to the Canary Islands and spent a warm winter there. They fell in love with the surreal landscapes of La Graciosa and the rugged volcanic island of Lanzarote. In the spring, they sailed to the Portuguese island of Madeira for a week of hiking. From there, they cruised to the Mediterranean, where they spent the summer months darting between the Balearic Islands, Sardinia, Corsica, and Sicily. Finding two refugees floating in the water off the Moroccan coast in harsh conditions was the most dramatic moment they have experienced with their yacht so far. Fortunately, they were able to rescue both of them.

In January 2022, Jessica and Jan set sail from Cape Verde to Martinique powered by confidence and a large amount of sourdough bread and salted pretzels.

The 2,100 nautical miles (2,420 mi/3,890 km) along the "Barefoot Route" across the Atlantic took them 17 days. They found their third crew member after making an appeal on Instagram. While Guillaume did not have any more sailing experience than the couple, his presence enabled them to split shifts three ways. Initially, the trio missed a perfect weather window due to illness and then started on an unforgettable adventure slightly later than planned. After navigating through some lulls, they sailed halfway into the middle of a threatening-looking cloud front. Thunder and lightning surrounded the *Adhara*. For safety reasons, they stuck their iPad, normally used for navigation, and their satellite phone in the microwave and took care not to touch any metal in the cockpit. For 24 hours, they motored through the low until it finally receded behind them, and they encountered the trade winds, which made for an easy journey toward the Caribbean in sunshine. It was an emotional moment for Jessica and Jan, arriving on a tropical island to the applause of friendly sailors—and as a newly engaged couple. "You see nothing but the blue expanse for two weeks, and suddenly you're catapulted into another world," says Jan.

We wanted to live with less and experience more.

Once again, volcanic islands captured their imagination—but this time in the Caribbean. They explored the paradisiacal landscape of their favorite island, Dominica, while canyoning, hiking, and free diving with a fellow sailing couple from Europe. The natural diversity of the Caribbean impressed them, especially after being greeted by an orca while on Guadeloupe. Some stretches reminded them of the rugged and rocky coastline of Brittany, France, and just a short time later, they hiked to a waterfall in a lush green tropical rainforest. On Antigua, an island in the Lesser Antilles, they got to know a variety of anchorages and woke up in a new place every day, surrounded by fine, white sand beaches and coral reefs.

Sometimes there are days when Jessica and Jan curse their boat and would swap their maritime life for their old comfortable life on land in a heartbeat. "But the pendulum swings both ways because every aspect of this lifestyle is much more intense. You can experience heaven and hell within a day, a few hours, or even minutes," Jessica says. However, the bluewater crew would not want to miss out on their new lifestyle. Nowhere else do they feel as alive as aboard their floating home. They dream about sailing in the Pacific someday—preferably with an addition to the family in the cockpit. ◂

BOAT FACTS Jessica and Jan searched for six months for a seaworthy cruising yacht that met their requirements. They visited trade shows, inspected different sailboats, researched online, and created lists of pros and cons. Their final choice was a luxurious 1998 Contest 48CS, which they christened *Adhara,* after the star of the same name. The *Adhara* is 48 ft (15 m) long and 14 ft (4.25 m) wide, with a 6 ft (1.8 m) draft. Apart from its solid construction, the model from the Contest Yachts shipyard in the Netherlands impressed the couple with its center cockpit, galley kitchen, spacious main cabin in the stern with a 5 ft (1.5 m) wide double bed, and the cutter rigging with two headsails. The yacht is equipped with a watermaker, a 165 gal (750 L) freshwater tank, 710 W solar panels, and a generator. In addition, the couple added two gadgets rarely found in long-distance galleys: a sparkling-water maker and a stand mixer.

The striking landscape of Gran Canaria, Canary Islands (right page). Jessica and Jan spent a whole summer exploring the Balearic Islands, including the fishing village of Fornells on Menorca (next spread, right page, top). The *Adhara* in a bay on St. Vincent in the Caribbean (next spread, left page, bottom). During their Atlantic crossing, the crew caught a mahi-mahi and made ceviche (next spread, right page, bottom right).

Jessica in front of a waterfall in Guadeloupe (this page, left). The crew spent a week hiking on the Atlantic island of Madeira (this page, right and right page, top), where they also visited the Botanical Garden (right page, bottom right). Snorkeling off the Mediterranean island of Corsica (right page, bottom left). The rugged landscape of the volcanic island of Lanzarote left Jessica and Jan spellbound (previous spread).

DIVING INTO AN ISLAND PARADISE

The Caribbean has captured the imagination of many seafaring nomads and is now home to a burgeoning boat-life community working, surfing, and flourishing among the palm trees and coral reefs.

DOWNSHIFTERS, DIGITAL NOMADS, couples on sabbatical, families on parental leave… people from all sorts of backgrounds will find plenty of kindred spirits in the Caribbean. The region is a firm favorite with sailors who live on their boats full-time, having left their old lives behind, whether for an extended break or forever. It is not uncommon for two or more sailboats to form a mini flotilla—the crews help each other out with boat maintenance and everyday necessities, while sharing the maritime spectacle drifting past their pulpits or playing out beneath their hulls. This part of the world has plenty to commend it to freedom-loving sailors: tropical temperatures, picture-postcard views of palm-fringed white sand beaches, warm turquoise seas, a vivid underwater realm, and favorable wind conditions. Thanks to the constant trade winds, the Caribbean is considered one of the most agreeable regions in the world for sailing.

Atlantic crossing adventure

For Europeans who aspire to make the Caribbean boatlife dream a reality, there is a thrilling yet eminently doable task ahead. But before adding snorkeling with turtles to the morning coffee-and-yoga routine, there's the matter of crossing the Atlantic.

Several hundred cruisers embark on this voyage every year. Vessels sailing from Europe to the Caribbean usually make the most of the trade winds to waft them from the Canary Islands to Grenada, Barbados, or Martinique between November and March. Known in German as the "Barefoot Route," this also marks the traditional start of circumnavigations from Europe. On their way to the Caribbean, many boat-lifers make a small detour to the Cape Verde archipelago off the northwest coast of Africa to replenish their supplies, fill up on diesel, make some final repairs, or pick up extra crew members for nonstop voyages lasting several weeks. Mindelo harbor on the island of São Vicente offers all this and is also the go-to place for those looking to hitch a lift on a boat. The roughly 800 mile (1,300 km) stretch from the Canary Island to Cape Verde is the perfect test of a sailor's skill and takes around a week on average, depending on the sailboat and the prevailing winds.

The most exciting—and longest—part of the Atlantic crossing starts from the Cape Verde Islands. The crews sail 2,000 nautical miles (around 2,300 mi/3,700 km) across the open sea, which is over 9,800 ft (3,000 m) deep in some places. This is a time for marveling at the vast blue expanse, gazing at the endless starry sky above the mast, perhaps getting stuck into a pile of books, and spotting marine mammals that, with a bit of luck, may even escort boats for hours. Even below deck, Jessica Schoeller-Szüts and Jan-Hendryk Büse, who live on the *Adhara* (page 78), a Contest 48CS, could hear the clicks of the killer whales following them on the Atlantic crossing.

Freedom the slow travel way

Most crews travel at an average speed of about 5 knots (5¾ mph/9.25 kph), about the same as a leisurely bicycle ride—,and catch their first glimpse of palm trees on the horizon after around 15 days. According to Jimmy Cornell, a Briton and one of the most experienced sailors in the world, long lulls or phases of weak wind are becoming ever more common due to climate change. Traveling to the Caribbean from other directions is not quite as comfortable, but it can be much quicker. Coming from the United States or the Gulf of Mexico means sailing against the prevailing wind direction.

The islands of the Caribbean are divided into the Lesser Antilles, the Greater Antilles (including Jamaica, Cuba, Hispaniola, and Puerto Rico), the Bahamas, and a few other islands. One of the most popular routes is in the Eastern Caribbean, down the Lesser Antilles, a rainbow-shaped archipelago that stretches all the way from Aruba in the south to the Virgin Islands in the north. Most of the 50 islands in this chain lie no more than a day's sailing from each other. Sailing to a different island often means having the gain entry clearance from scratch, as these are mostly independent island states. On almost every island they visited, the locals greeted Jessica and Jan-Hendryk with "Welcome to Paradise!" Sometimes, the Austrian and the German found themselves wishing that they had sailed these waters in the

Living on a boat in the Caribbean means waking up to views of palm trees, like here on the island of Antigua, or landing on a deserted island in St. Vincent and the Grenadines (left page).

days of Bob Marley, with reggae music wafting from the boomboxes at the beach bars rather than pounding techno. The infrastructure differs from island to island. On the Grenadines, for instance, food and diesel can be hard to come by and very expensive. Those who decide to go sailing here should be sure to stock up on plenty of food and fuel, ideally on the French islands.

Taking time out in the Antilles

Many sailors who live and work on their boats permanently look for secluded anchorages away from the tourist hotspots on the main islands and try to avoid overpriced marinas and charter ports. Hedvig von Essen and Mattias Wernersson from Sweden spent five months in the Eastern Caribbean on their yacht, *Monkii* (page 64). While plying the traditional route along the Lesser Antilles during the high season between December and May, they never had anchorages completely to themselves, but they did come across spots off the beaten track, with just a handful of other sailboats nearby. Their personal highlights included the small, uninhabited Green Island off the east coast of Antigua. They were able to anchor their 41 ft (12.5 m) yacht close to the shore and had the sandy beach all to themselves, with only turtles, stingrays, and numerous shoals of colorful fish on the coral reef for company. Green Island is so tiny that the couple could hike all the way through the small tropical forest to the other side. From the Lesser Antilles, the crew crossed over to the Bahamas and the Turks and Caicos Islands—a British overseas territory lying southeast of the Bahamas—before heading east from Bermuda across the Atlantic to the Azores and back to Europe. For Hedvig and Mattias, Mayaguana, the easternmost island in the Bahamas, boasted the finest bay in the Caribbean, with the brightest turquoise waters they had seen on their entire spell in this part of the world. From their yacht, they watched the marine wildlife swimming beneath. Upon going ashore in their dinghy, they found more tracks left by flamingos and lizards than by people.

Cruisers heading in the other direction—westward from the Lesser Antilles to the Panama Canal and Pacific—sometimes stop off on the San Blas Archipelago. This area is called Guna Yala by the indigenous Guna people, but travel magazines have also dubbed it "one of the last paradises on earth." If you were so inclined, you could make for a new island every day of the year—the archipelago has around 365 of them. Surrounded by coral reefs, these remote islands are the very stuff of adventure novels. Around 60 have authentic Guna villages of small huts, while a few have become daytrip destinations for tourists from Panama. Other islands in the archipelago have nothing but a couple of palm trees, as though simply waiting for someone to come along and string up a hammock. Needless to say, you will not find internet access, supermarkets, big hotels, or paved roads here. Instead, sailors can enjoy idyllic vistas dotted with bright starfish and the occasional visit from the Guna, who sell fresh fruits, fish, and sometimes even Coca-Cola from their traditional boats.

Reefs and underwater raves

Boat-lifers with a penchant for watersports can usually be spotted from the array of surf- and kiteboards neatly lined up on their decks like books on a shelf. Enormous reefs, sandbanks, and volcanic landscapes that extend underwater provide the ultimate in reef and beach breaks (waves that break over a reef or near a beach), while the trade winds along the east coast of the Lesser Antilles will gladden the hearts of kitesurfers. Indeed, the Lesser Antilles are a favorite haunt of surfers—period. Barbados, which boasts surfing spots on all of its coasts, is especially popular. Union Island in the Grenadines is another mecca for boat-lifers eager to kitesurf, wingfoil, and windsurf, while Dominica and the

Free diving straight from the boat: The vivid coral reefs and crystal-clear waters of the Caribbean are underwater playgrounds teeming with marine life.

The several-week voyage across the Atlantic to the Caribbean offers up a wealth of glorious natural spectacles.

Beach break: A bar on the little island of Bequia in St. Vincent and the Grenadines.

rainforested island of Guadeloupe are beloved by scuba divers and free divers. Having spent several months sailing the Caribbean in the *Navika,* Alexandra Lakin and Lars Sandved Smith chose Dominica as the place to build up their diving experience (page 70). "The Caribbean may have less cultural diversity than other sailing hotspots around the world, but you can't help but marvel at the incredible landscapes and underwater wildlife. There's so much more going on beneath the waves than there is in the Mediterranean, so activities like free diving and scuba diving are that much more thrilling," says Alexandra. The couple, who work from their boat, were most surprised by the good internet reception available almost everywhere in the Lesser Antilles, with only a local SIM card required.

Crews or solo sailors spending more than one season in the Caribbean usually look for a safe anchorage or berth in a harbor to see out the hurricane season from June to November. The islands south of St. Vincent are popular during this period—they lie outside the hurricane belt, and some insurance companies will cover storm damage incurred in this region. The crew of the *Beaver* (page 124) weathered the stormy season between St. Vincent and the Grenadines and Martinique before crossing over to the South Pacific.

Building a community among the palms

The Caribbean can feel a bit like a big floating commune to many sailors. "I love the sailing community in the Caribbean," says Hedvig of the *Monkii* crew. "It's a place where people of all different ages and nationalities come together and forge friendships." Platforms like Instagram and YouTube are not the only ways for Caribbean cruisers to stay in touch and arrange to meet up in bays. For some time now, likeminded oceangoing vagabonds have been connecting online and offline in the Caribbean and worldwide through collectives like Ocean Nomads and the Young Cruisers' Association.

SAILING THE ROUTE LESS TRAVELED

MANY SAILORS CHOOSE the Cape Verde Islands off the northwest coast of Africa as the starting point for crossing the Atlantic, bound for the Caribbean. The main island of São Vicente invariably serves as a stopover for these adventurers to stock up and make their final preparations before the big push. But Chiara di Prima and her boyfriend, Jason Beaufort, have avoided the established "Barefoot Route" so far; they prefer something less mainstream or pressured. For several weeks, they have been exploring the Cape Verde archipelago itself in their steel boat, the *Amanzi*. After that, they will head to West Africa and set a course for Senegal, Gambia, and Guinea-Bissau, where they hope to rivers and spot hippopotamuses and crocodiles. After several months of adventures there, they plan to cross the Atlantic, sailing westward to French Guiana or Brazil.

So far, Chiara and Jason have visited Sal and São Nicolau, two of the 15 Cape Verde Islands. The landscape reminded the 28- and 32-year-olds of the postapocalyptic action movie *Mad Max*. Due to the dry climate, the vegetation is sparse and desert-like, forming a striking contrast with the turquoise sea. "We discovered that the real beauty of the Cape Verde Islands lies in the bright and diverse realm beneath the waves," enthuses Chiara, an amateur free diver. Their favorite spot so far has been an anchorage off the secluded fishing village of Carriçal on São Nicolau, the greenest place they have encountered in Cape Verde. If traveling overland, the village can only be reached by a six-hour hike or an offroad drive. They settled down to read in hammocks strung between palms and acacia trees, visited every now and then by curious chickens and donkeys. The local people were very friendly and welcoming, and one of the village elders invited the couple into her little house. It was not long before the ladies of the village were teaching Chiara her first African dance steps. Both Chiara and Jason also tried the national dish, *cachupa*—a corn and bean stew. They found the island of Sal much more touristy, but still managed to find secluded anchorages and superb surfing and kitesurfing spots. At Monte Leão, they could paddle straight from their boat to a small wave just 650 ft (200 m) away.

For almost five years, Chiara, from Spain, and Jason, from South Africa, have been living on the waves, first on a 24 ft (7.3 m) Swedish monohull and, for the last three years, on the *Amanzi,* a 30½ ft (9.3 m) Buchanan Brabant with pale-red sails. Their adventure on the *Amanzi* began in England. From there they sailed to Brittany and crossed the Bay of Biscay to reach Galicia in northern Spain—sometimes accompanied by a large pod of pilot whales—before sailing down the Portuguese coast. From Portugal, where they adopted ship's cat Shaka, they crossed to the Canary Islands, before sailing onward to Cape Verde. Over the course of their journey, they were forced to take several breaks due to Covid-19 restrictions, the demands of their jobs, and some major refits of their roughly 60-year-old boat. Their all-time low came after a four-month refit. They were preparing to give the hull a coat of antifouling paint when they discovered a little blister which, after sanding down, turned out to be an enormous rusting hole. This calamity took them to the brink of giving up on their boat-life dream altogether. But after six arduous and emotional months, they were ready to set sail again.

They could paddle straight from their boat to a small wave just 650 ft (200 m) away.

For the past nine months, Chiara and Jason have been accompanied by a friend on their sailing adventures. They admit that it is not always easy to get enough personal space with three people, or even two, on a 30½ ft (9.3 m) sailboat. The key is for each member of the crew to do activities on their own. Jason heads out surfing or spearfishing alone at times, while Chiara does yoga, goes for a hike, socializes with the locals, or goes on photography excursions.

The couple dream of eventually sailing all the way to New Zealand, or perhaps even sailing around the world. As time has gone on, they have been trying to figure out how to finance their alternative lifestyle over the long term. Jason has worked on sailboats since his early twenties, while Chiara first signed on to a superyacht crew four years ago, and they have occasionally left the *Amanzi* to pick up this sort of work. These days, however, they are reluctant to interrupt their boat-life for the sake of jobs elsewhere, and are exploring ways of working from on board. Chiara has a degree in psychology and is currently training to become a personal coach. "Among other things, life on board the boat has shown us that many of our fears are undoubtedly fueled by society," says Chiara. We may not have bulging wallets, but we feel alive and healthy, and we're having the adventure of our lives right now."

BOAT FACTS *Amanzi* means "water" in Zulu, one of the national languages of South Africa. The Buchanan Brabant is 30½ ft (9.3 m) long and was designed by shipbuilding engineer Alan Buchanan. The hull of the steel boat comes from the Netherlands, and the vessel was completed in 1964 at the Scarr Shipyard in Goole, England. Chiara and Jason paid €10,000 (about $10,800) for their long-keel yacht and have invested a lot of time and money in refits since, including countless welding jobs on the deck and hull. Two 100 W solar cells and a wind generator provide the power. A water tank built into the keel can store 32 gal (120 L) of fresh water. They also have several canisters on deck that they can fill or use to catch rainwater. Below deck they have a cabin to themselves, and the saloon has another two berths. Five surfboards, five kites, two kiteboards, four harpoons, snorkeling and free-diving equipment, and climbing gear are also stowed away on board.

Chiara and Jason spent six whole months in the Canary Islands. The *Amanzi* at anchor in Los Gigantes Bay in Tenerife, beneath 1,476 ft (450 m) cliffs (previous spread). A hike amid the golden dusk on the island of La Graciosa (right page).

Adventure on the Cape Verde Islands: Jason goes surfing straight from the boat in Monte Leão Bay, on the island of Sal (this page). Hiking on the lush island of São Nicolau, with a view of Monte Gordo (right page, top). Jason in his element at the surfing spot of Ponta Preta on Sal (right page, bottom). Colorful fishing boats off the port town of Tarrafal on the western coast of São Nicolau (next spread). Everyday boat-life on the *Amanzi* (spread after next).

L 208

SAILING THE SCOTTISH HEBRIDES IN A CUTTER

IMAGINE A LANDSCAPE of rich green mountain ridges grazed by sheep, and deep bays hemmed in by steep cliffs—a place home to puffins, otters, seals, and dolphins. On land, white sandy beaches alternate with picturesque fishing villages and historic ruins. Scotland's rugged west coast is the happy roaming ground of the *Eda Frandsen*. This traditional sailing vessel, built in 1938 in Denmark, was used for cod fishing up until the 1980s. In the 1990s, the boat underwent an extensive refit and has been chartered out ever since. The two-person crew, consisting of Englishwoman Stella Stabbins and Scotsman Mungo Watson, has been running it as a business for two years. The couple loves taking people out into the great outdoors, expanding their horizons and sharing their own joy of sailing with others. The two sailors regularly open their floating home to guests in Scotland and Cornwall (far southwest England) and offer a glimpse of their way of life.

From May to mid-September, Stella and Mungo sail along Scotland's west coast, where the islands of the Outer Hebrides offer superb sailing. The Outer Hebrides extend some 125 miles (200 km) and are not overly developed for tourism; indeed, some of the islands are completely uninhabited. In these parts, the sea is often calm as a lake, as the archipelago offers protection from the rough Atlantic swell.

The couple spends April, September, and October in Cornwall, which captivates their guests with its cinematically stunning bays and rivers, not to mention its maritime history. Like Stella and Mungo, lots of people here live on a boat all year round. For some, this is due to a craving for an alternative lifestyle, but the worsening housing crisis in this region also plays a part.

In their adult years, Stella and Mungo have probably spent more time on water than on land. Both of them are certified Yachtmasters with considerable experience: before they took over the *Eda Frandsen,* they lived and worked full-time on other sailing vessels. Mungo grew up sailing and has been a crew member on countless superyachts. He has crossed the Atlantic and the Pacific multiple times. Stella came to boat-life a different way: although her parents took her sailing as a child, it was only during her university years that she discovered the books of famous circumnavigators such as Joshua Slocum and Bernard Moitessier, and was enthralled by their tales of adventure. She simply could not imagine living in a city and working in an office: "That sort of life didn't seem sociable or sustainable to me. I knew that I wanted to learn some practical skills and see more of the world," says Stella. She decided to sign on as a member of luxury yacht crews to gain the skills and experience she needed.

Stella and Mungo have sailed in many places around the world, including the Caribbean, the South Pacific, Russia, Central and South America, and New Zealand. Yet both of them are delighted their own business now ties them to Scotland and Cornwall, so that they can finally be closer to their family and friends, rather than a long-haul flight away. Nowadays, the most challenging passage for the crew is the stretch from Cornwall to Scotland—nearly 400 nautical miles (460 mi/740 km) up and down the Irish Sea between Ireland and Great Britain. During this voyage, keeping a close eye on the changing tidal currents is vital. "In sailing, there's no shortcut to picking up knowledge. Learning how different weather patterns behave and how boats can navigate different sea routes takes years," says Stella.

On one leg of a voyage, a minke whale surfed the bow wave of the Eda Frandsen for a whole hour.

Over the years, the couple have had more than their share of magical experiences, from seeing the Northern Lights to encountering orcas, being accompanied by bioluminescent dolphins while sailing at night, and watching little storm petrels frolicking around them during a violent thunderstorm. Yet more than any other, one moment remains imprinted on Stella's memory: watching a minke whale—probably a young male that wanted to play—joyfully surfing the bow wave of the *Eda Frandsen* for an hour as they sailed past the Isle of Man.

Unique moments like this mean much more to the couple than material possessions. Boat-life has taught them how to get by and be happy with minimal possessions, and that a willingness to be flexible is essential if you are to enjoy yourself on the waves. "Life at sea can be very unsettled. Jobs, situations, and plans can change rapidly for all sorts of reasons. You have to live in the moment and give it your all without getting too hung up on the future," says Stella.

BOAT FACTS The *Eda Frandsen,* a traditional shark cutter, was built in 1938 in Denmark from larch wood on an oak frame. The spacious sailing vessel does not look its age thanks to an extensive three-year refit in the 1990s by the previous family of owners. The 56 ft (17 m) boat is named after the wife of the Danish fisherman who owned it in the 1970s. Below deck, the *Eda Frandsen* has eight berths for guests and three for the crew. There are two bathrooms and a large saloon with a dining area and a small galley. The ship is traditionally rigged as a gaff cutter and does without modern aids like winches or furling systems. When in Scotland and Cornwall, it sails with a mainsail, topsail, staysail, three different-sized jibs, a jib top, and an asymmetric spinnaker for light winds.

Sunset in Kentra Bay, off the Ardnamurchan peninsula in western Scotland (right page, top). Typical Scottish seas on the voyage from Muck to Canna, both in the Inner Hebrides (right page, bottom left). Stella and Mungo serve sustainable local dishes, like scallops and mussels, aboard the *Eda Frandsen* (right page, bottom right).

View of the Cuillin Hills, a mountain range on the Scottish island of Skye, looking toward the *Eda Frandsen*'s anchorage on Loch Scavaig (left page, top). The sun sets behind the island of Rum (left page, bottom left). A puffin on Lunga, the largest of the Treshnish Isles (left page, bottom right). An anchorage with majestic views of one of the uninhabited Shiant Isles in the Outer Hebrides (this page).

A LIFE AT SEA IN PERPETUITY

SOME PEOPLE SPEND almost their entire lives sailing the oceans of the world. You rarely hear much about these wayfarers because, instead of investing precious time in YouTube videos and self-promotion, they live entirely in the moment, traveling to the remotest places on our planet, which often do not even have names, and setting sail according to the rhythm dictated by nature.

Denis Dowling is one of those people. The bearded American started his sailing career almost 20 years ago when he met a Greek skipper, who became his mentor and sailed with him from California to Greece. Since that unforgettable trip, Denis has sailed around the world on a variety of boats, first as a sailor and later as a captain. He has crossed the Atlantic eight times in his 40-year life to date and has clocked up over 150,000 nautical miles (172,600 mi/277,800 km) in his logbook. Ten years ago, the adventurer met his wife, Allison Medeiros, 33, in Newport, Rhode Island. Allison had just returned from a six-month solo voyage in New Zealand. They fell in love and undertook extensive long-distance cruises between the States, the Caribbean, and the Pacific before setting out on an expedition in the Mediterranean. For 18 months, they sailed there on a traditional wooden schooner, searching for remote destinations in the Aegean that were largely untouched by tourism. During that time, they sailed 3,000 nautical miles (3,450 mi/5,550 km) to more than 30 lesser-known islands in the Greek archipelago. This trip inspired them to buy their own sailboat and start a new chapter. For the past five years, they have been proud owners of the *Mr. Badger,* a classic 41 ft (12.5 m) oak and mahogany Concordia Yawl built in the 1950s, which they spent several years restoring.

Allison and Denis's home waters today are the New England coast in the northeastern corner of the United States. Their longest trip to date with their twin master took them from their home port of Jamestown in Rhode Island 1,000 nautical miles (1,150 mi/1,850 km) from their home port of Jamestown, Rhode Island, to Roque Island, Maine, and back. This route was rather short compared to previous trips but by no means less challenging. In the tide-dependent area, the crew had to sail with a lift of up to 39 ft (12 m) and the strong currents that sometimes resulted. In addition, these waters, also home to countless lobster traps, are frequently covered with dense fog that severely restricts visibility. Moreover, since they were sailing late in the season, they had to dodge several hurricanes and weather storms by taking refuge in anchorages and marinas. It is forbidden to land on Roque Island by dinghy, as the island is privately owned. So while they anchored in the fog off Roque Island, overlooking the long beach between towering pines and the small sister islands, they felt like they were in a fairy tale. "The island seemed like a fortress that once belonged to a long-forgotten pirate king," Allison remembers. Both are consistently fascinated by Maine's coast, which is home to black bears, puffins, moose, and humpback whales. One of their favorite sailing spots is the Merchant Row Archipelago consisting of dozens of small pine-covered islands with granite rock shores and offering secluded anchorages for both sailing and kayaking enthusiasts.

When they anchored off Roque Island, they felt like they were in a fairy tale.

The two boat-lifers agree that the most beautiful places they have experienced around the world in a sailboat so far have been remote corners where they have landed by chance thanks to storms or emergency repairs. One such place was Île-à-Vache, a small island off the southern coast of Haiti that measures only about 20 mi² (50 km²). "This island has been bypassed by the so-called 'progress' of society," Allison says. "There is no electricity or running water, and the island lives mainly from fishing the surrounding waters on small hand-built sloops called *batiman.*"

Allison and Denis financed the big refit by offering charter trips on the *Mr. Badger* in New England. Today, their full-time jobs include marketing a 30-year-old company that makes canvas tents—originally made for cowboys, now used by outdoor enthusiasts.

An evening walk lit by kerosene lanterns to the Moose Peak lighthouse on Mistake Island, Maine, USA (previous spread). Anchoring off Rhode Island and leaping straight into the sea: for Allison, this is the stuff that summer is made of (right page, top). Like onboard camping: Allison and Denis in their unusual sofa berths in the saloon (right page, bottom left). Denis (right page, bottom right) has been sailing for over 20 years.

The two have spent a lot of time working on boats in the past—for example, when it took them a few years to figure out what was causing water to enter their boat on a daily basis or why their engine never cut out at their home mooring, but always on longer trips. There is one key thing Denis has learned in almost 20 years at sea: "You will always encounter a surprise, face a new challenge or an unforeseen situation. You can work through all the checklists and instructions in the world, but at some point, you just have to cast off and go." ◄

BOAT FACTS *Mr. Badger* is a 41 ft (12.5 m) Concordia Yawl built in 1957 at the traditional shipyard Abeking and Rasmussen in Lemwerder, Germany. The elegantly furnished salon of the wooden twin master consists of a cozy sitting area adjacent to the galley. The unusual sofa berths fold out and transform the salon into a comfortable sleeping area at night. In the bow are two more folding beds and a small bathroom. During the refit, Allison and Denis removed some electronic equipment installed by previous owners and swapped the heavy diesel engine for a more compact Yanmar 3YM30. They obtain energy from a detachable 200 W solar array and store it in a portable lithium-based power bank (1,500 Wh). The power bank powers their camera equipment and electronics and charges two standard 12 V batteries for energizing the engine's start system. They store drinking water in simple water canisters.

On a deserted island in Maine, the couple pitched their tent with a view of the *Mr. Badger* at anchor (this page). In the pastel-tinged dusk, Allison photographs Newport Bridge in her native state of Rhode Island (right page, top and bottom left). Denis grills freshly caught lobsters on the beach (right page, bottom right).

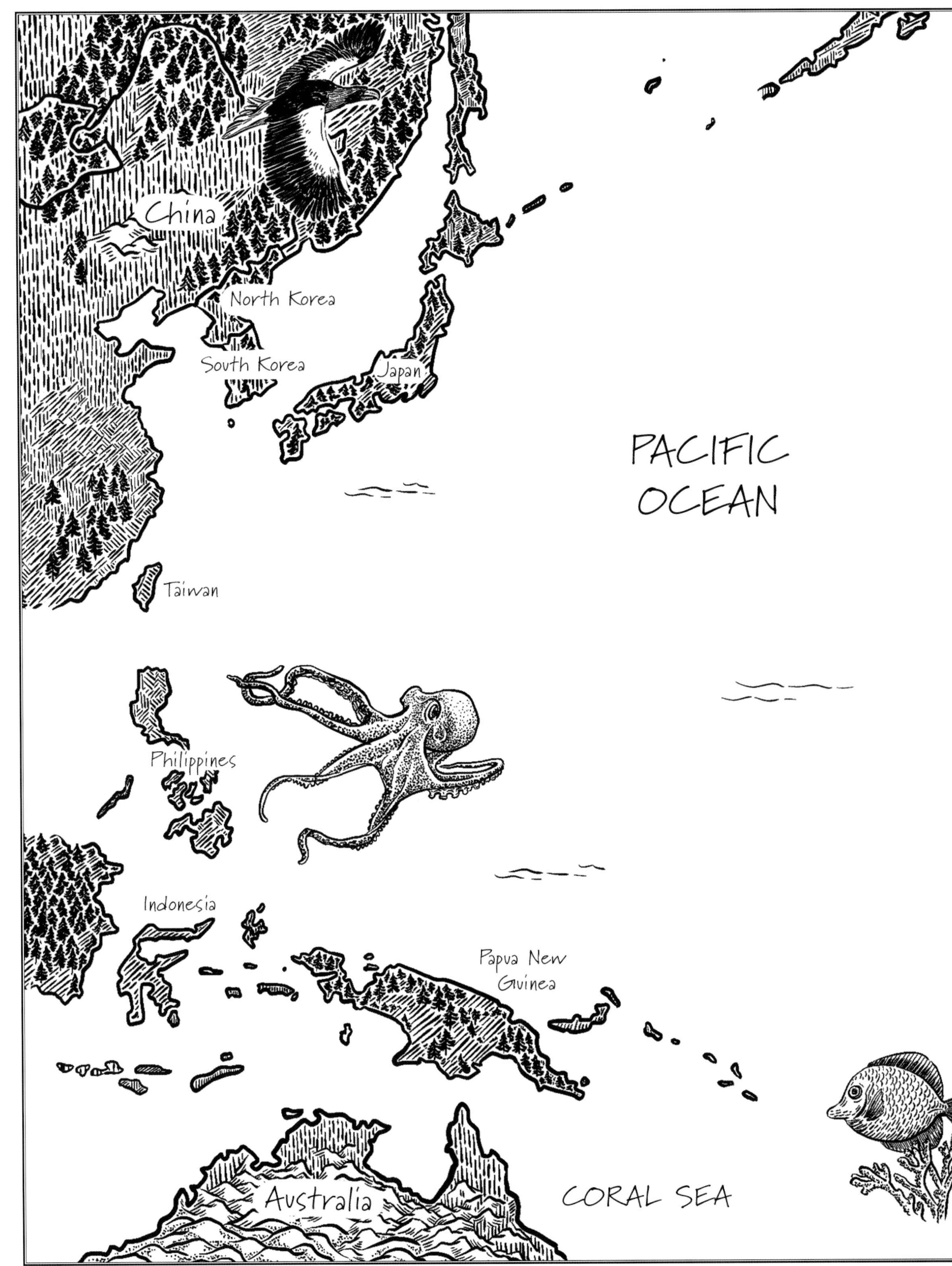
China
North Korea
South Korea
Japan
PACIFIC OCEAN
Taiwan
Philippines
Indonesia
Papua New Guinea
Australia
CORAL SEA

Canada
SALISH SEA
USA
SANTA BARBARA
CHANNEL
Mexico
Cuba
Guatemala
El Salvador
Nicaragua
Panama
Colombia
Ecuador
Peru
ench Polynesia
SOUTH PACIFIC
OCEAN

COAL

CALIFORNIA DREAMING ABOARD A SELF-BUILT WOODEN CUTTER

PHOTOGRAPHER and welder fabricator Nate Stephenson was lying in his bunk when he suddenly heard dolphins chattering next to him by the ship's side. Peering through the hatch into the darkness, he discovered an entire school swimming and chasing around his sailboat. Bioluminescence made the playful marine mammals and their movements in the water glow, making his first night aboard his floating home anchored in Santa Barbara, California, a magical start to a new chapter in his life.

Nate's unusual sailing story began six months earlier. Using a classified ad portal, he started looking for people who wanted to sail with him. He had no sailing experience and no money to own a sailboat either. The then owner of the *Mayfly,* which he now owns, got in touch and sent along a photograph of a wooden cutter. The two wrote back and forth, and surprisingly the owner offered to give the wooden cutter to Nate with the following words: "Whom better to give this boat to than someone who really wants to sail." There was only one catch: the owner had grounded the boat, and, exposed to the tides at anchor for several months, it now needed some repairs. Nate embraced the new challenge that life had thrown at him, and brought the wooden boat back to life. Among other things, the 27-year-old added an outboard motor that had not been there before. The Californian also installed a new rudder blade he built himself, additional solar panels, and a gas heater, and patched up the damaged keel.

As his wooden boat became more home-like, Nate decided to move out of the shared house he was living in. An adventurer who loved to travel the world alone in a car with a roof tent or as a hitchhiker, he had made himself comfortable within four walls for too long. He wanted to experience freedom at sea on the *Mayfly,* anchored in Santa Barbara, and find out whether life at sea suited him. The fact that he saved the monthly rent for his room in the house share was a welcome side effect.

When he's not doing repairs, Nate has been sailing his new home in the Santa Barbara Channel, a strait in the Pacific Ocean between Southern California and the offshore Channel Islands. His sailing area is about 80 miles (130 km) long and 10 miles (40 km) wide on average. In the future, he would like to make many trips to the eight Channel Islands together with his girlfriend, who now also lives on board, to further explore the partly sheltered waters of the archipelago, which are known for their abundance of marine life. So far, Nate has spotted white sharks, humpback and gray whales, seals and sea lions from the deck. "The Santa Barbara Channel is a dream to sail but not the friendliest place for a novice to learn," Nate says. After all, the channel crossing can be challenging, but there are many well-sheltered anchorages, which are not crowded despite their proximity to the mainland.

Nate only discovered the whole story of his *Mayfly* later. English boat builder John Lomos built the boat in Japan over several years, finishing in 2019, and then crossed the Pacific from Japan to California at the age of 79. For five months, he was stuck in a calm in the middle of the Pacific without an engine and almost starved to death. Shortly after he arrived in California, he had to fly back to England for personal reasons and handed over the *Mayfly* to the man who ultimately gave the boat to Nate.

Nate has spotted white sharks, humpback and gray whales, seals, and sea lions from the deck.

The photographer records his life on board exclusively with his analog camera. He likes this kind of photography for the same reasons that he likes sailing. "Both are slow processes. While most things in our world offer almost instant gratification, I like the delayed reward of analog photography and sailing. No rush, perfect imperfection, and limitless room for growth and experimentation," he enthuses.

He says he used to live much more in the future than the present, always thinking about tomorrow. "Then I realized that this is not a meaningful approach for me, and as clichéd as it may sound, I have since tried to live in the moment and do my best and keep my goals in focus. I want to be actively involved in what life has in store for me," says Nate. His wellbeing and enthusiasm continue to grow as he becomes more confident in his new way of life.

Once his monohull is ready for longer trips and Nate has developed his sailing skills, he wants to set off for Mexico with his pale blue wooden boat. Ideally, he would like to take this characteristic wooden cutter's builder, now over 80, on one last trip.

BOAT FACTS The *Mayfly* is a self-built wooden cutter, only 27 ft (8 m) long and just under 8 ft (2.5 m) wide. Nevertheless, it has five berths, a kitchen, and a wet room. It was cold-formed from Japanese cypress planks and marine plywood and covered with fiberglass. Its design is based on a James Cook by Glen-L, a U.S.-based company supplying boat plans for amateur builders. However, the builder of the *Mayfly* made many individual adjustments and adapted it to his needs for crossing the Pacific single-handedly. Right now, this sailing one-off is getting a major refit on land. Nate and his girlfriend are painting the hull, replacing the skeg and rub rails, and adding some lead ballast to the keel. They are also adding a bracket for the outboard motor.

Nate lives on his *Mayfly*, anchored in Santa Barbara, California. From there, he, his partner, and their friends regularly sail out to California's Channel Islands in the Pacific (previous spread, next spread, and spread after next, right page). His favorite place there is Santa Rosa Island, with its endless sandy beaches and diverse fauna (right page).

Nate captures his adventures on his 27 ft (8 m) long self-built log cutter with his analogue camera. A buddy of Nate's on the deck of the Mayfly (this page). Besides upgrading the exterior of the old boat, he has also given it a refit below deck, in pale blue (previous spread, left page, top left).

FOLLOWING THE "BAREFOOT ROUTE" FROM NORWAY TO NEW ZEALAND

CIRCUMNAVIGATING half the globe had long been Nicole Carlsen and Sam Hawkins-Pitman's dream. Sailing from Norway to New Zealand, the couple lived at sea for four years. Everything felt different when they returned to their old life in Norway by plane. "It's cold," Nicole says. "It's nice to experience the changing of the seasons again, and fresh, cold air in the morning is nice, at least for now," she adds.

Their big trip began with the purchase of a seven-year-old Beneteau Oceanis 40, which they christened *Beaver.* The then 26-year-old Norwegian and the 29-year-old Australian lacked any sailing experience. As a deck officer on supply ships, Sam had plenty of navigation experience but had never spent time on sailboats. In the winter of 2018, after a year of boat preparation for bluewater sailing, the crew of two cast off in Norway and first toured the Atlantic coast of Europe. A year later, they crossed the Atlantic from the Cape Verde Islands to Barbados in 16 days and then spent a year in the Caribbean. They weathered the hurricane season between St. Vincent and the Grenadines and Martinique to make the big push across the Pacific from Panama to the Marquesas Islands in French Polynesia in spring 2021—sailing some 4,000 nautical miles (4,600 mi/7,400 km) nonstop across the Pacific in 32 days.

For Nicole and Sam, the South Pacific was the most beautiful tropical sailing area on the classic trade wind route. At the Tuamotu Archipelago, the largest chain of islands in the world, they fulfilled their wildest dreams: they found remote atolls, secluded anchorages, and paradisiacal beaches where they often made campfires in the evenings. There were endless opportunities to pursue their hobbies of surfing and diving far away from mass tourism.

However, sailing between the hundred or so often deserted islands of French Polynesia also presented the crew with challenges compared to sailing in European or Caribbean waters. Since they did not have a watermaker on board to make fresh water from salt water, they sometimes had to manage for six to seven weeks with their 95 gal (360 L) freshwater tank and a few more canisters. And because the next boat shop with spare parts was often several thousand miles away, their improvisation skills were regularly in demand. On the other hand, they saw dolphins almost every day, had numerous encounters with whales, always had huge banana plants on board, and were overwhelmed again and again by the colorful underwater world of the tropics. They spent half a year exploring French Polynesia and Fiji and then spent six months exploring the North Island of New Zealand, to which they could easily cross thanks to the tailwind.

They found remote atolls, secluded anchorages and paradisiacal beaches where they often lit campfires in the evenings.

They preferred to stay in one place for at least a week. After a swim in the sea in the morning, they would start the day by doing some work on their laptops. They both occasionally worked en route to finance their adventure, although this cost significantly less than living on land in Norway. Nicole took on some translation projects, and Sam occasionally traveled to Australia to sign on as a deck officer on other ships. They used their afternoons to explore the islands, coastlines, or the underwater world. In the beginning, they sometimes wished they had a little more space and a washing machine on their 40 ft (12 m) boat, but the two temporary nomads managed to get used to that with time.

Nicole and Sam agree: if you want to live on a boat, you have to be flexible in terms of plans and adapt to what the weather and seasons allow, especially in the face of tropical cyclones. However, in stormy weather they also learned to stay calm, which proved to be a great mental and physical challenge for both of them at times. "But we managed to make ourselves comfortable even in uncomfortable situations," Nicole says.

Nicole and Sam weathered the hurricane season in St. Vincent and the Grenadines (previous spread and next spread). Namotu Island, one of the islands of Fiji, is surrounded by idyllic surfing and diving spots (right page, top). From her hammock, Nicole enjoys the views of the hilly west coast of Raiatea, one of the Society Islands of French Polynesia (right page, bottom left). The *Beaver* at anchor in the remote Tuamotu Archipelago, French Polynesia (spread after next).

Since they were on one of the typical bluewater routes, they met many other sailors, with some of whom they formed close friendships. At sea, they kept in touch with other boat-lifers mostly via satellite phone or email. After their unforgettable period of life at sea, Nicole and Sam are certain that they will always live on or with a boat in the future and stay connected to sailing. They sold the *Beaver* in New Zealand. They are currently looking for a new boat that can withstand sailing in the Arctic and enable them to experience adventures in cold climes. Svalbard, the home of polar bears, is their next destination. ◀

BOAT FACTS The *Beaver,* an Oceanis 40, was built by the French sailboat and motorboat manufacturer Beneteau. The spacious cruising yacht is 40 ft (12 m) long and 13 ft (4 m) wide. Nicole and Sam found the white seagoing vessel online and bought it in Portugal. Its name is a nickname of a deceased friend of the two. The boat has three cabins, a 53 gal (200 L) diesel tank, and a 95 gal (360 L) water tank. During their four-year cruise, Nicole and Sam had the sails overhauled and bought more sails second-hand, among other things. They renewed all the electronics and installed a wind generator, a wind control system, and four 110 W solar cells to enable them to navigate the world's oceans comfortably and independently of shore power.

ADVENTURES IN THE KINGDOM OF THE HUMPBACK WHALE

RACHEL MOORE has been living on a Tayana Vancouver 42 sailing boat for the past six years with author Joshua Shankle. "The last four years have been the best of our lives so far," says the photographer. Originally, the two Americans wanted to take five years to sail around the world together. Their voyage began in 2016, leaving from California, sailing to Mexico, and then from El Salvador to Panama and the Galapagos Islands. They finally crossed the Pacific in 27 days to reach French Polynesia. They wanted to spend a year in the French overseas territory of more than 100 islands. They've now spent four years there (and counting), and their boat named *Agápē* has long been their floating home. "We decided that we wanted to make sailing our lifestyle and not a trip with an end date," the 33- and 36-year-olds explain. They no longer intend to circumnavigate the world but want to get to know places in their own time, dropping the anchor wherever it takes their fancy and then sailing on when it feels good.

The warm, crystal-clear water, the extraordinary underwater world, numerous near-deserted islands and atolls, great surfing and diving spots, and the locals' remarkable affinity with nature fascinate the couple. "Polynesian culture regards the size of your smile as more important than what you have in your bank account," Joshua adds of this paradise in the middle of the Pacific they currently call home.

They only head for ports when they want to fly to see their families; otherwise, they usually anchor on their own in a quiet lagoon protected from the swell by a coral reef. It is no rarity for them to be able to see the ocean floor from their boat. In French Polynesia, they live much more comfortably than in other areas with rougher seas they have already explored. However, navigating atolls can be very challenging because many lagoons are unmapped. They usually use satellite imagery, and one of them will stand at the bow or on the spreaders, keeping an eye out for coral heads lurking just below the water's surface that could damage their hull.

Whether snorkeling, free diving, or scuba diving, the couple spend almost as much time underwater as they do on the boat. French Polynesia is one of the few places in the world where diving with whales is allowed, albeit subject to certain rules. Every year, hundreds of humpback whales are drawn to the blue lagoons between late July and early November to give birth to their calves. Rachel and Joshua spend this time in the waters around the heart-shaped island of Mo'orea, northwest of Tahiti. Rachel is in the water almost daily, swimming with and photographing the giants, which can measure up to some 60 ft (18 m) in length. "Some days, the whales are very inquisitive, especially the playful calves," she says. Tour guides who have become good acquaintances are often there as well.

Around Mo'orea there are impressive coral gardens with huge reefs of rose-shaped coral plates at a depth of about 65 ft (20 m). "The deeper reefs are healthier than the shallow-water reefs, which have been affected by bleaching, pollution, and agricultural runoff," Joshua says. At the south pass of Fakarava, an atoll in the Tuamotu Archipelago about 310 miles (500 km) northeast of Tahiti, the two long-distance sailors have swum several times with hundreds of gray reef sharks, colorful reef fish, manta rays, hammerheads, tiger sharks, and whale sharks close to their boat. The reef has been listed as a UNESCO World Heritage Site since 1977 and is in excellent condition.

Rachel is in the water almost daily, swimming with and photographing the giants.

However, paradise can sometimes turn into a nightmare. In their first year, the crew of two was surprised by a storm in a lagoon. Without any prior warning, the wind started blowing from the opposite direction, causing a 6½ ft (2 m) wave to build up and their anchor to work itself loose in up to 40-knot gusts. It took considerable effort over several hours with the engine running to keep their boat from being pushed onto the shore. "Our lifestyle can be exhausting, frustrating, expensive, and restrictive—but it can also be the exact opposite," says Joshua. It allows them to live as economically and ecologically responsibly as possible. "When I was still working in California, I was totally stuck and didn't even realize it," the sailor recalls. "When you're living the typical American dream, you might spend most of your life working for a lifestyle you never really cared about."

The crew has since expanded to three members. Gilly, a street cat, has grown up on the *Agápē* and loves dinghy tours and devouring fish and coconut milk. Rachel and Joshua dream of buying a bigger boat one day to accommodate their families and friends on board for long periods. They also want to explore the Indo-Pacific and its underwater worlds with their sailing home. ◀

SAILOR'S NOTES: ONBOARD DIVING EQUIPMENT

After completing several intensive courses, Rachel and Joshua are now scuba and free-diving experts, allowing them to explore the underwater world independently without a dive guide. The couple has two complete sets of scuba and free-diving equipment on board the *Agápē,* including special diving goggles and carbon fins. Six years ago, the two invested in a breathing air compressor (MaxAir 35) to fill their tanks, which they have used to fill more than 600 tanks on board, enabling them to dive even in the most remote places. They attach the tanks to the mast while sailing and stow the remaining equipment below deck to protect it from the sun. They use action cameras and a high-quality SLR camera with underwater housing for underwater shots. Rachel makes the following recommendation: "Always dive with a dive buddy, stay within your comfort zone, and let someone know beforehand where you are going to dive. Safety first!"

For four years, Rachel and Joshua explored French Polynesia on *Agápē,* a Tayana Vancouver 42 (previous spread). When the Covid-19 pandemic broke out, they were not permitted to leave this atoll in the Tuamotu Archipelago (right page)—far away from civilization, without internet, and with just two friendly crews from neighboring boats.

From their anchorage in Mo'orea, Rachel and Joshua head out in their dinghy to find diving spots amid the nearby coral gardens (left page). Joshua searching for coconuts in the Tuamotu Archipelago (this page, left). The couple's favorite activities include free diving with humpback whales, oceanic whitetip sharks, and blacktip reef sharks in French Polynesia (next spread).

CRESSI

Surfing and scuba diving are Joshua's favorite activities in French Polynesia. Besides pristine beaches, this spot is also renowned for its perfect reef breaks (this page). Anchorage with a view of Mount Mouaroa on the island of Mo'orea (right page). Joshua up a coconut palm and Rachel at the campfire—both on remote islands in the Tuamotu Archipelago, French Polynesia (next spread).

LEARNING TO LIVE WITH LESS AT SEA

Moving onto a boat usually means living in a smaller space and doing without certain things. To be long-term happy with this new way of life, it is worth creating as much space as possible below deck.

MORE AND MORE people are now rethinking their old way of life and opting for a scaled-back version of the home, in the form of a microapartment, van, tiny house ... or boat. In the West, downsizing and "small living" are becoming increasingly popular alternatives and routes to a sustainable lifestyle. People are doing without material things quite deliberately, rather than out of necessity. This minimalism serves as a kind of tool for leading a meaningful life, a bit like mindfulness or meditation. "All these things feed into the common goal of identifying what's really important, what truly counts. It is about defining yourself by who you are, not what you own," says professor of psychology Friederike Gerstenberg. It all adds up: those who live lavishly, consume a lot, and own a great many things need plenty of money to do so. That means that they need to work more, are under greater stress, and have less time for themselves and living their lives. Getting off that hamster wheel requires courage, self-sacrifice, and flexibility, but it is also a huge privilege—you get to decide how you want to live.

Goodbye, apartment—hello, boat!

Very few of today's boat-lifers have always led a completely minimalistic life. Prior to their life on the water, many of them lived in room shares, apartments, or family homes. At a certain point, however, they decided to leave their old lives behind. Quitting an apartment lease, selling all their belongings, or putting a few prized possessions into storage and leaving the rest behind represents a kind of liberation for those who choose to start living on a boat, but it would be unthinkable for many of their acquaintances. In our achievement-obsessed society, we are always receiving the message that we need more and more in order to be happy. We are constantly hankering after more space, more possessions, more money, more success. As people grow their families, they start to need more space. Salary increases can often lead to "lifestyle creep," too. Capitalism thrives on our tendency to try to buy happiness. But there may come a day when you realize that this is not the answer. You may find yourself looking at things in a new light and turning toward a more sustainable alternative lifestyle instead. Also, people who consume less generally have a lower carbon footprint.

Your floating studio apartment

Once you have made the decision to live on a boat, you are soon confronted with the constraints of living in a tiny space, with very little storage room for superfluous things. Unless you are investing in a multimillion-dollar luxury yacht, a catamaran, or a spacious but stationary houseboat, your space below deck generally resembles a small studio apartment. The interior of a monohull vessel usually has a fixed layout, with most of the space given over to the sails, engine, freshwater, graywater and diesel tanks, anchor chain, repair materials, and stowage for provisions. The galley kitchen is integrated into the central living space, known as the saloon. In many cases, the cabins will be no bigger than the mattresses within them. A small bench is the onboard version of your comfy, inviting sofa, while the wet room with integrated shower is usually tiny. Only a lucky few boat-lifers will have proper headroom, space to walk around the table in the saloon, or a place to practice yoga below deck.

Pared-back living like this usually means fewer clothes, kitchen gadgets, and toys. Instead of a playroom brimming with playthings, children on board will usually have to get by with just a box of their favorites. In place of material possessions, however, they get to enjoy unique experiences. Children will grow up with an ever-changing front yard in some of the most beautiful places on earth, with endless possibilities and priceless experiences. They get to live a life in harmony with the elements—the great outdoors is their playground. In the words of American publicist Arthur Buchwald, "The best things in life aren't things at all." Academic studies have shown that spending money and time on experiences rather than objects pays off, because experiences linger in our memory for longer and lead to a more lasting sense of happiness.

Sustainability and self-sufficiency

Boat-life offers a high degree of self-sufficiency and low carbon footprint, giving young people all the more reason to swap their lives on land and take to the waves. Electricity comes from solar cells, a wind generator, or a hydro unit; watermakers transform seawater into drinking water on well-equipped boats; salt water can be used to flush toilets, and the power of the wind alone propels you all over the world. "These days, it's clear to many people that we're in the middle of climate change. We're polluting our planet with waste. Our species can't go on like this much longer," says Professor Gerstenberg. "A desire to lead a minimalistic life often goes hand in hand with a striving for sustainability." This might sound simple, but it can often pose considerable challenges, not least when your next harbor is hundreds of nautical miles away, your watermaker is on the blink again, you barely get to see the sun while sailing in Arctic waters, or the wind is not turning the blades on your generator as it should. When living on a boat, you soon get to know your daily energy and water consumption, and naturally adopt a more mindful approach to resources and the environment. In other words, you begin living more sustainably, budgeting better and

Lots of crews carry watersports equipment on board. Australian Hayden Greener loves exploring the Great Barrier Reef with diving gear or his e-foil board.

being more inventive, especially when you end up in remote places. You can bathe in the sea and use canisters to collect rainwater. You end up saying goodbye to things that consume a lot of power, or not taking them on board in the first place. Anything that gets broken has to be repaired using what you have on board, rather than thrown away—acceptable replacements are often very difficult to come by. You get a better sense of how much waste you produce, too, as you cannot simply toss your garbage into a bin and forget about it; instead, you have to wait until you go ashore to dispose of it. When you see plastic floating in the sea or lying on beaches on a daily basis, you develop real scruples over excessive packaging and automatically start seeking out local produce, ideally plastic-free.

From Lego to little luxuries

But even boat-lifers do not travel merely with the bare essentials for survival, such as basic provisions, safety equipment, and materials for repairs. Take Lily Mercieca and Hayden Greener, who have been sailing Australia's Great Barrier Reef for three years on their 40 ft (12 m) yacht (page 148). They would not dream of doing without their diving and watersports gear. "Our love of adventure inspired us to take up this lifestyle," they say, "so we make sure we have everything on board to make the most of it." When it comes to onboard luxuries, a few things come up time and time again: smartphones, camera equipment, laptops, books, aquatic gear, ski equipment, yoga mats, espresso makers, Lego, barbecues, sewing machines, and bicycles.

Working from home, boat-life-style

Embracing boat-life does not have to mean cutting ties with mainstream society. Nowadays, those who move on to their boats often choose to work remotely as a way of supporting their lifestyle, saving up for retirement, paying for their insurance, funding any repair costs, and providing them with the wherewithal to fulfill their dreams. According to careers platform Zippia, the number of people working remotely has quadrupled over the last four years in the United States alone. In the wake of the Covid-19 pandemic, working from home has gained new popularity and status, making this type of work and relocating to your own boat office all the more appealing. The life of a digital nomad suits people from all manner of professional backgrounds, including creatives, entrepreneurs, engineers, coaches, and freelancers—all you need is a laptop and a good

More and more people are now working remotely, making doing your job from a boat more popular than ever. Swedish sailor Lars Sandved Smith is doing his doctorate from his cabin in the Caribbean.

Most long-distance sailors equip their boats with solar cells and a wind generator.

internet connection. True, you will not find the latter in the middle of the Atlantic or Pacific, but you can access the web from near the coast using local SIM cards, port networks, or satellite internet, which has recently become much more affordable. There are plenty of boat-lifers who earn money offline, too. They dock at ports and spend a period of time working ashore, perhaps as nurses or mountain guides; earn money by transferring other boats from place to place; or charter out their own berths.

Maintaining your personal space on board

Living and working within a small space can sometimes leave you with very little room for yourself. Landlubbers often puzzle over how crew members cope with living in such cramped quarters. But many people do not mind the restricted space. According to Laura Ritthaler, psychologist and author of the book *Emotional Detox,* this also has to do with how we were raised. As children, each of us has different amounts of space to roam around in. The less space you had to yourself and the more you had to share with others, the more space and time you crave for yourself as an adult. Everyone who has spent a long time living on a boat agrees that teamwork and openness are the key to living harmoniously with several people in a small space. "It's worth bearing in mind that we can also create space for ourselves by attending to our personal equilibrium," says Ritthaler. She advises couples and families living on boats to establish routines where all crew members do things on their own at regular intervals and invest in at least 15 minutes of self-care every day.

Minimalism can be physically and mentally freeing. Those who opt to live on a boat are usually prepared to downsize, let certain things go, and adopt a whole new outlook on life. In return, they can look forward to unforgettable adventures on the oceans, very special memories, and the kind of freedom that money cannot buy.

SAILING AMONG CORAL REEFS AND CROCODILES

THE GREAT BARRIER REEF is the biggest coral reef in the world, stretching over 1,240 miles (2,000 km) along Australia's east coast. It is so enormous that it can be seen from the International Space Station. Somewhere amid the thousands of reefs and islets are Lily Mercieca and Hayden Greener in the *Haven,* their 26-year-old Concept 40 sailboat. In all likelihood, they are in complete isolation out there, with no other boats in the vicinity, no internet access, and no mapping. Yet being in the midst of an underwater realm teeming with life and color is ample compensation. The 26- and 30-year-olds have made Australia's east coast, and the Great Barrier Reef just offshore, their own personal playground for almost three years. The two Australians rave about gorgeous sandy bays, lapped by crystal-clear azure waters and surrounded by coral gardens, of venturing out to the edge of the reef, where the seabed drops some 6,560 ft (2,000 m), and of the richly diverse marine life that they get to experience almost every day. They have witnessed dolphins playing around the bow, spotted clownfish and seahorses swimming among soft and hard corals, seen giant turtles nesting on the beach, free-dived to watch whales and manta rays, and heard humpback whales and their calves singing. And they have had more fearsome encounters, too: they once came across crocodiles unawares at the outermost reaches of the Great Barrier Reef.

As a rule, this two-person crew spend six to eight months away from civilization before heading to a port to stock up on provisions. Before they depart from the mainland again, Lily and Hayden preserve, freeze, and pickle as many fruits and vegetables as they can. They also stockpile lots of canned goods for emergencies. And their self-sufficient approach does not stop at solar cells and wind generators: they try to eat mainly fresh food while on the *Haven,* by fishing, harvesting coconuts, gathering wild sweet potatoes and various types of algae, and growing sprouts and herbs on board. They have even tried their hand at growing mushrooms and spirulina, a type of microalgae. Their water supply comes from collected rainwater and their watermaker. "The downside of desalinated water is that minerals are removed along with the salt. We add trace elements to counteract that effect. We also drink fresh coconut water, which contains natural electrolytes," says Lily.

Despite their isolation, the couple do sometimes meet like-minded sailors. On Lizard Island, they were delighted by the pristine natural beauty and by the sailing community they found there. With their newfound friends, they whiled away the days with tai chi, yoga, birdwatching, slacklining, hiking, and playing the guitar. They also learned how to surf with an e-foil (an electric board) and visited a research station on the island. "The island felt like a local school, with everyone sharing their favorite skills and pastimes," enthuses Lily.

These two boat-lifers usually spend six to eight months away from civilization at a time.

Such things come easily now, but making this their way of life was far from easy. For a long time, Lily and Hayden lacked the financial means to buy their own sailing yacht. They toiled away at tough jobs and endured a great many hardships over the years in order to fulfil their dream. These days, their biggest challenges are the tropical storms, cyclones, and strong currents that sailors face in this part of Down Under. On one occasion, while anchored in a lonely bay for the night, their vessel was caught in a sudden storm with winds of up to 70 knots (80 mph/130 kph). Within the space of a few minutes, *Haven* had been gusted from its anchorage onto the sandy beach. It was a huge shock, but luckily the boat was unscathed. The couple could not help but smile when they looked out from their unconventional berth to see a crowd of curious ghost crabs peering at them. The tide came in the next morning, carrying their 40 ft (12 m) hull back out to sea.

As everyone is aware, the Great Barrier Reef is currently blighted by coral die-off due to climate change. Although the two Aussies have known about this since they were little, the speed at which coral bleaching is occurring never ceases to shock them. Along with coral die-off, the vast expanses of garbage that wash up from the oceans and become caught on the corals and beaches are a massive issue for this sensitive habitat. Mindful of doing their bit, Lily and Hayden collect garbage on almost every dive or beach walk. They also report and document coral health on behalf of a clutch of organizations.

As the couple cannot surf in the Great Barrier Reef, they are eager to go looking for remote reef breaks in the South Pacific. "When we find them, we'll jump straight off the stern of our yacht, paddle out, and go surfing nonstop," laughs Hayden. ◄

SAILOR'S NOTES: MIDDLE PERCY ISLAND—A SAILING HOTSPOT According to Lily and Hayden, stopping at the iconic Middle Percy Island is an absolute must for anyone sailing down the east coast of Australia. In the right conditions, West Bay makes a superb spot for casting anchor, swimming, and hiking. On the ravishing beach stands a palm-fringed open hut that locals have nicknamed "The Percy Hilton." Over the years, this hut has evolved into a museum of yachting memorabilia. Hundreds of plaques and curios display the names of the ships and crews that have stopped here. Newcomers have the opportunity to immortalize their own sailing feats in this collection by adding a memento. This spot also boasts a camping kitchen, barbecue, shower, bathroom, and a little stall selling local produce. "It has the best honey in Australia. There's a firepit behind it, too, where adventurers from all over the world meet up to chat, laugh, and have a singsong," says Lily.

Lily and Hayden watched humpback whales from Dolphin Point on Hayman Island, in Australia's Whitsunday Islands (previous spread). The crew on their spacious Concept 40, called *Haven* (right page, top). Hiking on Langford Island (right page, bottom left), a popular spot for anchoring, snorkeling, and diving (right page, bottom right).

The Australian couple relaxing in a bay on Lizard Island, in the Great Barrier Reef, which can be reached only by boat (left page, top). A healthy reef in the Great Barrier Reef (left page, bottom). Hayden in Mossman Gorge, Daintree Rainforest, Australia, one of the oldest rainforests in the world (this page, left). Sunset on the sandy beach on the edge of Daintree Rainforest (this page, right). Four Mile Beach in Port Douglas (previous spread).

patagonia

FROM SOLO SAILOR TO ENVIRONMENTAL ACTIVIST

SOLO SAILOR LIZ CLARK is a role model for today's generation of sailing enthusiasts. Some 17 years ago, at the age of just 25, this U.S. sailor departed from her home port in California aboard *Swell,* her 40 ft (12 m), 1966-built Cal 40. Having studied for a degree in environmental studies, Liz has a deep awareness of the massive destruction of the planet at the hands of humankind, and this had completely turned her off the consumption-driven American lifestyle. "I wanted my way of life to reflect my love and respect for the planet," she says. So she set sail without any specific route in mind, but simply with the dream of finding the most remote surfing spots in the world and achieving a more sustainable way of living. Now 42, Liz was one of the first single-handed sailors in the world to blog about her life on her boat and post about her doings on social media. Having since become a published author and sailed over 20,000 nautical miles (23,000 mi/37,000 km), she still receives countless messages from people—especially women—who have similar passions or who aspire to emulate her feats in the male-dominated world of sailing.

At the age of just seven, Liz learned to sail a small sabot. When she was 10 years old, she and her parents made a six-month voyage from California to Mexico. After this family trip, during which she was struck by both the beauty and the fragility of nature, two things were clear to her: she needed to protect the environment from the destructive urges of humans, and she wanted to captain her own sailboat one day. After graduating from university, she was assisted in this ambition by a friend and mentor who bequeathed her his old boat. She spent three years repairing it and outfitting it for a long-distance voyage. Ever since Liz was small, her father had also been encouraging her to pilot and repair their family sailboat. She was inspired by adventurers like Tania Aebi, who sailed around the globe in two years in the mid-1980s, becoming the first and youngest U.S. female circumnavigator.

Liz started off by spending a year and a half sailing along the coast of Mexico and Central America, before crossing the Pacific from the Galápagos Islands to the Marquesas Islands. Her mother accompanied her on the 3,300 nautical mile (3,798 mi/6,112 km) crossing to this archipelago in French Polynesia, an overseas collectivity of France in the South Pacific, made up of several hundred islands stretching over 1,240 miles (2,000 km). This tropical paradise fascinated the nature lover so much that she postponed her plans to circumnavigate the globe. Once she had had her fill, Liz went on to sail the South Pacific alone for over a decade. With her were 10 surfboards; her adopted stray feline companion, Amelia the Tropicat; and the occasional bouts of seasickness that plagued her in rougher seas. On her travels, she explored many of the islands and atolls of the Tuamotu Archipelago and the Society Islands. "I learned to love being alone," says Liz. In fact, as she was constantly working on her boat, writing, or surfing, she had very little time to feel lonely. And if feelings of lonesomeness ever crept up on her while at sea, she would turn to her favorite books and spiritual teachings, which helped her keep negative emotions at bay. On other occasions, she would seek out contact with other boat-lifers or locals.

Sailing solo helps me to find my center again.

It was only after many years of sailing alone that Liz started to wish she could share her adventure with someone. She now lives on Tahiti with her husband, Tahui. The couple met in 2015 while Liz was writing her memoir of the voyage, and had a traditional Polynesian-style wedding in 2022. But Liz has not completely forsaken her seagoing ways for life on land. Her boat lies anchored very close to where she lives, and she still ventures out in it alone every now and then. "Sailing solo and surfing both help me find my center," she says.

Liz now dedicates much of her time to animal welfare and marine conservation in the South Pacific. The nonprofit organization that she works with, A Ti'a Matairea, has prompted local people to set up marine sanctuaries in eight overfished lagoons. Another initiative enables volunteer vets to assist with the sterilization of the many stray dogs and cats in these parts. These days, the activist has a whole host of new dreams: to keep making a difference, to grow her family, to create an idyllic home with a lush garden, and to surf the perfect waves. And there are sailing plans in the offing, too—this time with Tahui and, of course, a few four-legged friends on board. As far as Liz is concerned, being out at sea and relying solely on nature and her own wits remains one of the most thrilling experiences imaginable, and one that is hard to come by almost anywhere else in the modern world. "I'm glad that I was so determined to follow my dream of sailing," she says. "It forced me to face myself and find out what I'm made of. I'm a much happier person now than I was back then."

SAILOR'S NOTES: SUSTAINABILITY ON THE *SWELL* Protecting the oceans is very important to Liz, who knows only too well that it is impossible to be 100 percent sustainable when sailing, even on your own boat. She makes her own cleaning and hygiene products and uses local coconut oil for everything from skin moisturizer to cooking oil to lubricant for tools and teak. She mixes up her own all-purpose cockpit and cabin cleaner from vinegar, water, a dash of biodegradable detergent, and a drop of essential oil. Her toothpaste is made from baking soda, peppermint, and coconut oil. She also uses a mineral sun cream that is free of ocean-harming ingredients like chemical UV blockers or nanoparticles. When shopping, she is careful to buy products with as little plastic packaging as possible. If she does end up with any plastic, she makes sure that it gets repurposed—as a trash bag, for instance. "I believe we can all make choices in our daily lives that reduce our impact on our environment, our oceans, and wildlife," says Liz.

Surf spot in Mexico (right page). The Marquesas Islands (next spread, left page, top left). Solo sailor Liz does the dishes, watched by curious reef sharks (next spread, left page, top right). Surfing off the Line Islands (next spread, left page, bottom). The swell at anchor off a palm-fringed atoll in French Polynesia and a successful fruit harvest in Tahiti (previous spread and next spread, right page).

FROM BRITISH COLUMBIA TO THE SHORES OF MEXICO

SOMETIMES THE EXPERIENCES of our childhood go on to shape the course of our entire lives. That was certainly the case for Kayleen VanderRee. Kayleen, now 30, grew up on a sailboat. When she was a little girl, she and her parents sailed to Canada. As a teenager, she accompanied them on a longer voyage to Mexico—a journey that changed her whole perspective on life. After completing a degree in marketing, she knew that she wanted to continue with this alternative lifestyle instead of joining the rat race. Inspired by her own friends and female sailors like Liz Clark, who sailed the Pacific solo (page 156), the young Canadian bought her first sailboat and started planning an offshore trip alone. Then, in 2017, she met Tyler Turner on a dating app, and to her surprise, she quickly gained another crew member.

Tyler, an athlete, grew up on the Canadian Prairies—about as far from the coast as you can get—and had only done some occasional lake sailing aboard Hobie Cats (lightweight catamaran sailboats). But from his and Kayleen's very first date, there was no denying the sparks between the old salt and the landlubber. At that time, Kayleen was selling her first boat, and the couple were soon making plans to buy a floating home together—a Jason 35. For two years now, they have been living on an altogether more spacious Tartan 42, a bluewater cruiser. They christened their vessel the *Footloose* in honor of Tyler, who lost both of his lower legs in a serious skydiving accident in 2018.

Tyler's new condition did not hold either of them back from sailing, not least because Kayleen knows the west coast of Canada like the back of her hand. These unique waters are rough, remote, and wild, but rich in culture nevertheless. New anchorages, snug little bays, and vast fjords await around every corner. Temperatures range from 14 to 86°F (-10 to +30°C). Kayleen and Tyler have sailed through snow and hurricane-force winds in winter, but on warm summer days the sea can be as gentle as a duck pond.

Their favorite sailing spot is around the Campbell River and the Discovery Islands, an archipelago between Vancouver Island and the British Columbia mainland. The northern Discovery Islands are somewhat cut off and sparsely populated, but Kayleen and her 34-year-old boyfriend can always head to the southern isles for their fill of indigenous culture and history. Nearby, on British Columbia's Sunshine Coast, lies Desolation Sound, where clear waters are ringed by precipitous, evergreen-clad mountains—a veritable El Dorado for sailing, swimming, and snorkeling. The landscape is teeming with orcas, sea otters, black bears, and wolves. This sound is also home to one of the couple's favorite anchorages, and they have spent many a happy hour at the foot of the waterfall in Teakerne Arm inlet.

The landscape is teeming with orcas, sea otters, black bears, and wolves.

"Our life on board is this wonderful mixture of exhilarating and blissfully relaxing," says Kayleen. The couple's lifestyle has made a ship's electrician, diesel mechanic, fiberglass specialist, and woodworker out of her. "When it comes to living on a boat, sailing is just one part of the picture," she explains. Her main source of income is her work as a professional diver and freelance author. Tyler, meanwhile, leaves the boat for the snowboarding season, spread over two months of every year, to scoop up medals all over the world. As a paralympic gold medalist in snowboard cross, he is always looking for his next adrenaline rush. The couple's home port of Campbell River offers plenty to satisfy their love of sports, from snowboarding, skydiving, sailing, and fishing to winter surfing.

Following two years of preparation, they recently cast off from that haven and embarked on their first long voyage together, all the way to Mexico. It was not all smooth sailing: they hadn't traveled farther than Oregon on the west coast of the United States before they encountered difficult conditions. The sea became very rough, and Tyler had a bad fall. He had problems moving and trouble sleeping. The couple were exhausted, and Kayleen was wracked with guilt. Life on the boat has its ups and downs, and they sometimes find themselves questioning the path they have chosen. Ultimately, though, their optimism wins out, and they conclude that they have made the right choice. They do not take life too seriously: instead of wanting to be the best at everything, it is about having fun and enjoying the good times.

Looking to the future, they can see themselves on a catamaran, which offers a higher level of comfort. That said, Kayleen is not ruling out sailing around the globe. "I can imagine the older me as someone like Jeanne Socrates," she says. Jeanne Socrates holds the record as the oldest woman to sail solo around the world. To top it off, she is also the only woman to circumnavigate the globe nonstop starting from North America. ◂

BOAT FACTS At the height of the Covid-19 pandemic, Kayleen and Tyler were browsing a listed ads website when they spotted their spacious Tartan 42, built at Sparkman & Stephens shipyard in the United States in 1981. The *Footloose* was selling for around C$62,000 (around €43,000). They had to act fast: bluewater cruisers were in hot demand worldwide. The sails and rigging were in tiptop condition, but the couple still had to put in a lot of work to get their new adventure boat exactly how they wanted it. Among other things, they upgraded the entire 12 V system; installed a 700 W solar system; modernized almost all of the pipework, safety equipment, and ropes; replaced the anchor; and installed a wind steering device. "We've definitely gone over our initial budget, but you have to bargain for surprises when you buy an old boat," says Kayleen.

In winter, Kayleen and her friends go on splitboard and ski trips from their Tartan 42 (right page and next spread, right page, bottom).
In summer, she and Tyler explore the countless secluded bays and fjords (next spread, right page, top and spread after next) or find an anchorage with a view of the Vancouver skyline (next spread, left page, top).

Greenland
DENMARK ST
LABRADOR SEA
Canada

ARCTIC OCEAN
Svalbard
NORWEGIAN SEA
Norway
United
Kingdom
Sweden
Finland
Denmark
BALTIC SEA
NORTH
SEA
Russia
Germany
Poland

A FAMILY AND THEIR GREENLAND WILDERNESS ADVENTURE PLAYGROUND

EMMANUELLE DUMAS, Christophe Votat and their two children, Raphaël, 5, and Jade, 3, are a family with an appetite for adventure. "We are just normal people who like to do crazy things," says Frenchwoman Emmanuelle. She first met Christophe in Chile back in 2014. Emmanuelle had just returned from a four-week ski expedition in Antarctica, where she had worked as a guide. He arrived in port after an equally long leg on his boat along Chile's southern coast. They fell in love, and a short time later Emmanuelle moved onto Christophe's *Venus* without any prior sailing experience. A few years later, their son was born, and four years ago, just before their daughter was born, they bought a large aluminum boat, *Lifesong,* a Garcia 68 from the 1990s.

Boat-life enables the 34- and 39-year-olds to combine parenting with work without having to give up daily adventures in nature. The family has been almost everywhere in the world, but they have been sailing and living mainly in the northern latitudes since 2019. Norway, Greenland, and Svalbard take it in turns to be their adventure playground. During the season—from February to September—they often offer expeditions lasting several weeks, giving guests an insight into their experiences and everyday boat-life. Ski tours, glacier expeditions, kayaking, and hiking are on the daily itinerary. There are endless opportunities for outdoor enthusiasts beyond the Arctic Circle, especially in the summer, when the sun never sets. What fascinates the couple most about cold climes is how many places they have to themselves. Nature is unspoiled, and most of the time they are the only boat at an anchorage. The pastel-colored light and ever-changing ice landscapes inspire Emmanuelle to paint in watercolors.

Greenland is their favorite temporary home. For two seasons, they've explored the waters west and south of the vast island with *Lifesong,* and they cannot wait to sail along the northeast coast. But there are dangers lurking in Greenland, too. There is a lot of drift ice, especially on the east coast; the crossing from Europe can be dangerous, and in some places it is difficult to find fresh food. Emmanuelle advises sailing newcomers to the Arctic to visit Svalbard first. "There's not much drift ice here, you only have to travel short distances to get to new places, and you can find everything for your daily needs in the capital, Longyearbyen," she says. "The most inconvenient thing is that you have to carry a gun everywhere to protect yourself from polar bears."

Many outsiders may think that full-time boat-life with kids sounds impossible. Emmanuelle's response, on the other hand, is resoundingly clear: "Just do it! Kids can do anything; they adapt to the crazy sailing life, even in the Arctic. It's a great way for them to learn, grow, and meet very different people." She has sailed the oceans both heavily pregnant and with infants. Raphaël is homeschooled by his parents. They also have the support of someone on board to assist them with the children, cooking, sailing, and the various expeditions they lead for their guests. When sailing in rougher conditions, the children stay below deck. They don't get seasick, and can play Lego there, watch movies, or watch the waves roll by through their windows from their beds.

Kids can do anything; they adapt to the crazy sailing life, even in the Arctic.

Before having children, Emmanuelle and Christophe had frequently sailed on the opposite side of the globe. There, they have sailed the Drake Strait together, which lies between the southern tip of South America and the northern tip of Antarctica and is considered one of the most dangerous stretches of water in the world. Few sailors venture on this leg. Emmanuelle still remembers the moment they set sail for Antarctica in their boat at the time. The sea was rough, and in every direction the thick fog hid icebergs, which they could only see on their radar. Suddenly, the fog disappeared and the sun came out. The huge icebergs, against which the waves broke loudly, piled up right in front of them and curious penguins cavorted around their boat. "Antarctica is breathtaking—it feels like you're on another planet. The animals aren't afraid of humans—everything is pristine," Emmanuelle enthuses. The crew needed glacier gear for every stop ashore, and almost every anchorage was exposed to ice, requiring ice watches each night in the midnight sun.

Boat-life is not always easy for the family. Sometimes Emmanuelle and Christophe dream of warm temperatures, of having more time to themselves while the kids go to school, or of a smaller boat that needs less work. "But really, we have the perfect life, and I know I wouldn't want it any other way. It's hard, almost every day, but we love it," Emmanuelle says. ➤

BOAT FACTS *Lifesong* is an aluminum sailing yacht built in France. It is 68 ft (20 m) long and 16 ft (5 m) wide, and it has four spacious double cabins with bathrooms; a large salon with u-shaped kitchen and spacious seating area; two cockpits; and plenty of storage space for kayaks, the dinghy, skis, and the family's remaining outdoor equipment. The insulated boat is equipped with a twin heating system and water heater, double-glazed windows, and crash boxes designed to protect the hull when it comes into contact with ice. Emmanuelle and Christophe stow welding equipment, a sewing machine, and numerous spare parts on board to repair the boat and sails in the remotest of places. They produce fresh water with a watermaker (33 gal/150 L per hour) and use a generator, a hydrogenerator, and their diesel engine to produce energy. The diesel is stored in a 395 gal (1,800 L) tank.

This family of four (right page, bottom right) is currently plying the waters around Norway, Greenland, and Svalbard. The *Lifesong*, a Garcia 68, in May, in a secluded bay against the formidable backdrop of Svalbard (next spread).

Drift ice and icebergs on the doorstep: the *Lifesong* in Disko Bay on the western coast of Greenland (left page and this page).

MIDWINTER TO MIDSUMMER TO THE NORTH CAPE

KATHARINA CHARPIAN and Axel Hackbarth are living proof that spur-of-the-moment ideas can lead to thrilling adventures, especially on little-sailed routes. They had only been together for half a year when they decided to sail to the Norwegian Arctic in Axel's sailboat, the *Zest,* and back again—a six-month journey. Axel, a 38-year-old engineer at the time, wanted to take a career break and have a proper think about his future, while Katharina, a 34-year-old journalist, was able to run her former online magazine while at sea. Axel was used to dealing with all sorts of mishaps at sea like mast and rudder break, but Katharina's only experience of sailing was with him.

Their choice to set sail for the north in December 2020, in the dead of winter, raised some eyebrows. Even local sailors tend to avoid going to sea at this time of year due to the strong winds, the extreme cold, and some treacherous passages along the way. But the lovebirds were delighted that this adventure would take them out of their comfort zone. Before they could embark, the *Zest* needed an upgrade to equip it to cope with the wintry conditions. Axel had owned the 1986-built fiberglass Beneteau First 345 for 12 years, having pooled money with two friends to buy it. He and Katharina installed a secondhand oil stove and insulated the front berth. Merino long underwear became an essential part of their layered daily look. As there was no hot-water boiler on board, hot showers were reserved for stops at the few harbor facilities that remained open, or with water from the stovetop kettle.

The couple did not set out to follow a fixed route, but they did have a milestone in mind: they wanted their 34 ft (10 m) yacht to cross the Arctic Circle by early April, so that they could sail beneath the Northern Lights, experience the long days of sunshine, and celebrate midsummer under the midnight sun—north of the Arctic Circle, the sun never dips below the horizon from mid-May to mid-July. After a five-day crossing from Germany, the Endless Sunshine Sailors, as they call themselves on Instagram, arrived in Kristiansand in southern Norway. Just a few days later, the area experienced an unexpectedly severe cold snap, and they had to resort to fenders and boathooks to free themselves from the frozen harbor basin. Katharina and Axel sailed north up the coast through skerries and sounds, past snow-covered beaches, mountains, and thousands of islands. Along the way, they explored the Hardangerfjord, Norway's second-longest fjord; sailed 110 miles (180 km) through it to reach the town of Odda; and visited the island of Utsira and the Sunnmørsalpene mountain range.

They anchored right in front of a calving glacier at the end of the sparsely populated Jøkelfjord.

They crossed the Arctic Circle on April 9. On April 14, having traveled some 1,000 nautical miles (1,150 mi/1,850 km), they reached the Lofoten Islands just in time for the return of the puffins. On many a night, they anchored beneath the Northern Lights. They have a particularly fond memory of anchoring in the tiny fishing village of Å on the Lofoten island of Moskenesøy, with the Northern Lights dancing, all brilliant green and shimmering purple, right above their heads and the red stilt houses. From the Lofoten Islands, they sailed past the island of Senja, stopped in the city of Tromsø, and climbed peaks in the Lyngen Alps in northern Norway. The northernmost point in their journey lay just a day's sailing from the North Cape of Norway, and it could hardly have been more spectacular: the sailors anchored right in front of a calving glacier at the end of the sparsely populated Jøkelfjord.

All of the equipment they would need for adventures on the water and snow was stashed in the aft cabin, so the couple could enjoy the forces of nature on and off the boat. Having their ski gear close at hand meant that they could set off straight from the shore and climb mountains beneath the midnight sun, catch some Arctic waves on their surfboards, or speed over the small streets on their trusty longboards. Axel also experimented with his snowboard and a kite on daytime hikes. Their blow-up unicorn, *Rainbow,* completed the motley assortment of items on board.

Beachside houses in the fishing village of Bleik on Andøya, north of the Arctic Circle, reminded the couple of colorful Lego houses (right page). Caribbeanesque views on the island of Senja, northern Norway: the *Zest* at anchor amid the magical light of one April night, while the crew cooked a vegan barbecue on the beach and drank in the views of the snow-covered mountains (previous spread).

Their return journey was restricted to a window of just four weeks, so they sailed all night and all day, interrupted only by walking stops for their dog, Helle. In June, they experienced the summer solstice atop a rocky island right on the Arctic Circle. Accompanied only by a few birds—the usual denizens of the island—they celebrated the longest day of the year with wildflowers in their hair, the soundtrack from their Bluetooth speaker, and views of the *Zest* bobbing at anchor beneath the golden midnight sun. By the end of their epic 3,000 nautical mile (3,450 mi/5,550 km) Arctic quest, they both had answers to the question that had taken them there. Now they could picture a way of living and working that would satisfy them. A year after their return, they gave up their apartment in Hamburg and bought their co-owners out of the boat. Today, they are back out on the Atlantic Ocean near Spain with their dog, sailing and working as they go—heading for Patagonia.

SAILOR'S NOTES: SAILING AND SKIING IN NORTHERN NORWAY Anchoring in a fjord or bay, landing a dinghy on a snow-covered beach, and donning your ski gear to hike from the waterline to a mountain peak, before gliding down over powdery snow to your sailboat—you can do all these things in northern Norway, especially between February and May. With the help of various alpine-sports and weather apps, Katharina and Axel searched out potential peaks, researched climbing options, and checked for any risk of avalanches—all from their boat. In Tromsø, they met a family of eight who were big fans of ski-and-sail trips and passed on a lot of useful tips. Besides their touring skis, their equipment also included avalanche gear, a survival bivouac bag, a satellite messenger, and sufficient provisions. The couple were usually out and about for eight to twelve hours a day, and always had the mountains to themselves. Highlights included the 2,172 ft (662 m) Gavltinden, on Andøya island in the Vesterålen archipelago.

At the northernmost point of their journey, they anchored beneath a glacier at the end of the Jøkelfjord (this page). Boat office under the open sky in northern Norway (right page, top). The saloon, with views into the front cabin (right page, bottom left). The Lofoten Islands in April (next spread).

ADVENTURES IN THE LAND OF THE ORCAS, NORTHERN LIGHTS, AND SNOWY PEAKS

HUNDREDS OF ORCAS migrate to northern Norway between November and January every year. They follow the migratory patterns of herrings to the Norwegian fjords, where they hunt them in large groups. One of the best expanses of water for spotting orcas amid their spectacular natural surroundings is around Skjervøy, an island community on the northwest coast of Norway, not far from the North Cape. This stretch of sea is also the home and playground of 30-year-old Spanish marine biologist Inaki Javier Tomey Roca. Free diving with the black-and-white marine mammals ranks among Inaki's top ever experiences as a sailor. "Diving with orcas is almost impossible to describe," he says. "Being in the water with the most majestic creatures in our oceans is truly humbling." Inaki fell in love with the higher latitudes during his master's degree in Tromsø. Today, he lives and sails in the Arctic, usually in the company of his dog, Chester, and various researchers or curious visitors from all over the world. His company, MarineWide, offers regular sail-and-ski or sail-and-climb adventures and scuba diving trips from his floating home. From his home port of Tromsø, he sails out in his Grand Soleil 46, *Makaira II,* carrying small groups to the north of the Vesterålen archipelago, to Senja and Troms, or on explorations of the Lofoten Islands, which number more than eighty.

In Norway, the mountains and the sea are right next to each other, so skiing is a very special experience indeed. "It's a unique landscape, with colossal mountain peaks over 4,600 ft (1,400 m) high, towering straight up from the sea," he says. "It's nothing like skiing in the Alps." Once the boat reaches its destination, Inaki drops anchor and leaves it in a sheltered place, often a snowy bay. He then boards the dinghy with the crew and their skiing equipment, and they start their ascent straight from the water's edge. One of Inaki's favorite mountains for ski tours is Uløytinden on the island of Uløya. Climbing this 3,655 ft (1,114 m) peak affords adventurers spectacular views over the surrounding fjords and mountains, followed by a thrilling descent on powdery snow all the way back to the boat, for a well-earned night's sleep beneath the Northern Lights. Northern Norway—especially the Lyngen Alps, where Inaki's expeditions take place—are no place for novice skiers. There is a high risk of avalanches, so you need to know exactly what you are doing. This is one of the reasons why Inaki's friend Kevin Ochoa joins most of the one-week expeditions. As the first officer, he assists with preparations for the voyage, helps to cater for the guests, and leads trips into the mountains.

In summer, when the snow melts in the mountains, Inaki and his crew head up there with climbing ropes. The Lofoten Islands are an absolute mecca for climbing enthusiasts. One of Inaki's favorite climbs is Hermannsdalstinden (3,376 ft/1,029 m) on the western side of Moskenesøya island, just far enough away from the more famous Reinebringen. "You get breathtaking views of Værøy and the Reinefjord without people swarming all over the mountain," he says.

Free diving with the black-and-white marine mammals ranks among Inaki's top ever experiences as a sailor.

The Norwegian winter is peak sailing season for the crew of the *Makaira II*. Besides the cold, strong currents and the many shallows, one of the biggest challenges with sailing at high altitudes is the ever-changing wind. Due to the topographic relief of the fjord, the wind is constantly changing direction and speed, so Inaki has his work cut out keeping the boat on course. The ropes on board are often frozen solid, so there is nothing for it but to douse them with boiling water. It is just as well that Inaki loves a challenge and getting out of his comfort zone. No other lifestyle would come with such endless scope for personal growth and self-fulfillment. As a marine biologist, Inaki is particularly concerned with protecting the oceans. Over the last two years, he has teamed up with volunteers and Norwegian environmental organizations to clear more than two hundred beaches of plastic waste. He is also the founder of the Clean & Climb Initiative.

For the first few years, Inaki lived on his monohull full time. These days, having adopted Norway as his new homeland, he usually spends the winter in a small apartment in Tromsø, so as to maximize onboard space for trip preparations and equipment storage. He believes that living on the boat has fundamentally changed him. "You start to appreciate experiences more than material things. Minimalism is the key to a happy life on board." Greenland, Iceland, and the Northwest Passage are still on his bucket list, and he dreams of entering the Golden Globe Race one day. His experience diving with orcas and sailing in Arctic waters could make him a serious contender for the solo around-the-world race. ◂

BOAT FACTS The *Makaira II*, a Grand Soleil 46 built in 1985, was designed by Alain Jezequel and constructed at the Cantiere del Pardo shipyard in Italy. The expedition boat is 46 ft (14 m) long and has a large galley kitchen, two wet rooms with hot showers, and three cabins that can accommodate seven people. The spacious salon seats nine at its round bench and table. "If you're sailing in remote regions, it's vital to be self-sufficient," says Inaki. He has equipped the boat with a 185 gal (700 L) water tank, three solar panels (two 120 W and one 185 W), and a wind generator (400 W) to cope with long trips. The boat has been upgraded with insulation for sailing at high latitudes, while the independent diesel heater can heat the entire boat, including the cabins.

Captain and boat-lifer Inaki charts a new course on his chart table (right page, bottom). The northern fjords of Norway are said to be among the best places in the world to observe orcas (next spread, right page, top). During the winter months, Inaki sails into these waters in his yacht and goes diving with the fascinating marine mammals.

CRESSI

The *Makaira II* at anchor near Tromsø beneath the magical Northern Lights (this page and right page). Striking out from the dinghy (previous spread, right page, bottom right) and heading up to a mountain peak (previous spread, right page, top) before gliding down over the powdery snow amid a landscape of majestic fjords, with your sailboat at anchor below (previous spread, left page)—ski trips straight from a sailboat make for a unique experience in northern Norway.

ADVENTURES BEYOND THE ARCTIC CIRCLE

Sailing in the Arctic or Antarctic can stimulate the senses—cracking ice, looming icebergs—but the intrepid are rewarded with challenge and achievement in these untouched expanses.

SOME SAILORS fall in love with sailing in places where few dare to venture—around the ice-capped poles of our planet. Norway is the perfect training ground for newcomers to sailing in colder climes. Sail northward from Europe in winter and cross the 66th degree of latitude (more commonly known as the Arctic Circle), and you find yourself in a whole other world. Snowcapped mountains tower out of the water like giants, their tongues the frozen waterfalls that carve their way into the ink-black rock. By night, the Northern Lights dance over the mast, while orcas in the fjords feed right next to your floating home. Katharina Charpian and Axel Hackbarth experienced all these sights on their winter adventure on *Zest,* their 34 ft (10 m) boat, where they live and work (page 180). The couple set sail from Germany in December, bound for a challenging yet magical voyage north. The best time to see the

Northern Lights is during the darkest months of the year, from October to March.

Norway's winter wonderland

The infrastructure in northern Norway keeps ticking over even in winter: smaller harbors are usually closed, but those in larger towns remain open. Sailors can request a hot shower or a top-off with fresh water here. Supermarkets are open at regular intervals along the coast for stocking up on provisions, and fueling stations for local fishing boats are open all year round. It is best to pack some long merino underlayers, but the temperature rarely plummets too low. The Gulf Stream ensures that the country has mild winters all the way up to the North Cape, so harbors on the western coast of Norway stay free of ice in winter. Temperatures are generally between 14 and 41°F (-10 and 5°C), and only fjords that penetrate far inland tend to freeze. In those parts, the harbors are often equipped with technology that keeps mooring places from freezing over.

One of the biggest challenges with sailing at this time of year is the katabatic winds—cold pockets of air that descend rapidly and without warning from the surrounding glaciers into the fjords, like avalanches. Some sea passages, such as the area around the Stad peninsula or Hustadvika, are also considered especially dangerous in winter. The full force of the oceans meets an area full of shallows and tiny islets here, so navigating the waters requires a crew on top of its game.

Many Norwegians hold off sailing until the summer, so it was not until May that the crew of the *Zest* met a few kindred spirits from France, Germany, and Spain in Tromsø harbor. This Arctic city, just 200 nautical miles (230 mi/370 km) from the North Cape, is also the home port of the crew of converted lifeboat *Stødig* (page 202). Guylee Simmonds and David Schnabel, who work from their boat, like to sail over to one of the surrounding fjords in the early months of the year and head up into the mountains for skiing, straight from their boat. Besides watching orcas, sail-and-ski trips like these are among the reasons why skippers like Inaki Javier Tomey Roca find themselves drawn to the far north (left page and page 230).

From mid-May to around mid-July, the sun never sets above the Arctic Circle. In the summer months, the fjords, fed by glacier water, are reasonably free of ice. In those conditions, fiberglass boats can also venture into this rugged landscape—it is no longer the sole preserve of the aluminum or steel boats that predominate at the higher latitudes. Such trips often include voyages with views of the snow-covered Lyngen Alps, with gentle breezes, or hiking in the perpetual sunshine on the Lofoten Islands—at day or night.

Setting a course for Svalbard and Greenland

Tromsø is a popular starting point for crews looking to cross over to Svalbard on trips lasting several weeks. This archipelago lies halfway between the North Cape and the North Pole. In early July, Kika Mevs and Daniel Deckert crossed the Norwegian Sea from Tromsø to Svalbard in four days in their Pearson 36, a journey of just 550 nautical miles (about 630 mi/1,020 km) (page 230). The former mining outpost of Longyearbyen is the largest settlement on Svalbard. For some years now, the town, which is also accessible by airplane or cruise ship, has been morphing into a major tourist center, so most sailors only dock here to stock up on provisions, obtain fuel, or do their laundry at the marina. It is a different story in winter: the sun never rises on Spitsbergen, and with temperatures as low as -13°F (-25°C), ice floes take the place of sailboats in the fjords.

Norway, Svalbard, and Greenland have been the haunt of Emmanuelle Dumas, Christophe Votat, and their children, Raphaël and Jade, for three years. The family live on their aluminum cruiser *Lifesong* (page 172), a Garcia 68. Raphaël and Jade are growing up amid polar landscapes and glaciers. This crew found the Caribbean and French Polynesia too warm for their taste, but they loved the cold air and untrammeled nature of the northern climes. Greenland is their favorite playground yet, and they have already explored parts of the south, east, and west coasts by boat. During the summer, the temperature does not usually fall below 32°F (0°C) in Greenland, and sometimes it is well above that. With a bit of meditation, visitors can take an icy dip in 37°F (3°C) water. The crew almost invariably had Greenlandic anchorages to themselves, from where they could go hiking, skiing, or kayaking to places unreachable by another other means.

Those who want to experience the Antarctic with a minimal environmental footprint can join the crew of the bark *Europa*.

24/7 surrounded by ice

Ice is both the ultimate thrill and the ultimate enemy of sailors who want to experience the Arctic or Antarctic in their own boat. In the worst-case scenario, a bad collision could damage the boat so severely that it sinks. Periods of bad weather can be particularly challenging for crews, who have to battle strong winds and distinguish mini icebergs weighing tons—known as growlers—from the white crests of waves. Most sailors who head to these parts have boats equipped with radar systems, but they still have to keep active watch and take turns watching for ice from the bow or a spreader through the day and night, whether they are sailing or at anchor. Even for the experienced *Lifesong* crew, who have sailed near both poles, zigzagging around the many growlers in polar waters gets the adrenaline racing.

Such difficulties are compounded by the fact that some regions of the Arctic and Antarctic are inaccurately mapped or do not appear on charts at all. The crew of the *Ju Mar* had to contend with this very issue. Niklas Marc Heinecke and Joscha Brörmann were actually sailing toward the Caribbean, but rather than choosing the conventional route with a stopover on the Canary Islands, they chose to travel via Iceland, Greenland, and the east coast of the United States (page 220). In the Denmark Strait and Labrador Sea, the friends faced winds of up to 45 knots (52 mph/83 kph) and 26 ft (8 m) waves. They came to expect constantly reefed sails and seasickness on their voyage. Yet the experience that Greenland offers after an often rough crossing from east or west more than makes up for such hardships. They are greeted by surreal icy landscapes, lonely anchorages shared only with whales and polar bears, and magical sunsets in pastel hues. And the constant soundtrack of the Arctic ringing in their ears—the loud cracking of ice on repeat.

People who have lived on a sailboat for several years or even decades, exploring many parts of the world during that time, often begin by dreaming of sailing the wild and remote Northwest Passage. The 3,800 nautical mile (4,370 mi/7,040 km) route runs along the southern coast of Greenland and then across the north coast of Canada to Alaska, and is only navigable in the Arctic summer. Up here, at the very edge of the world, you are often in a race against the ice, as the various passages may become blocked by pack ice due to the weather, and cold snaps can stop you in your tracks with little notice. Nowadays, however, forecasts by satellite phone and the ever smaller ice cap on the Arctic Ocean due to climate change are making this stretch less and less dangerous than it was just a few decades

Power-napping on the ice: sailors in the Arctic or the Southern Ocean have a good chance of glimpsing seals, polar bears, whales, and penguins amid the frozen landscapes.

Arctic explorers will encounter increasingly fewer signs of civilization as they head farther north. The colorful Inuit village of Aappilattoq lies at the southern tip of Greenland.

ago. Meanwhile, only a tiny number of sailing crews per year have the opportunity to sail along the Arctic coast of Russia on the Northeast Passage (for political reasons), the shortest maritime route between Europe and Asia.

Ahoy, Antarctica!

Just as with the two passages around the North Pole, those who fancy sailing amid penguin colonies near the South Pole will need a highly experienced crew and a large, oceangoing boat made of aluminum or steel, with extra stowage for provisions, big water and diesel tanks, and double heating systems for weeks of voyaging in glacial seclusion. Antarctica's main sailing season lasts from November to March. When the sun returns, the sea ice retreats and the winds blow less fiercely. One of the few dozen sailing vessels that ply these waters every year is the bark *Europa* (page 208). This striking three-master crosses the notorious Drake Strait between South America and Antarctica several times during summer in the southern hemisphere. "It's much more difficult to get information about Antarctic sailing than Arctic sailing, but most sailors share their knowledge and support one another," says Emmanuelle of the *Lifesong* crew. As she tells it, being in the Antarctic felt like her family had landed on a completely different planet. She did not want her life story not to include an amazing South Pole adventure, and she was amply rewarded for taking up the challenge.

sunflare
iNavX
LOCHIN
ASAP

CROSSING THE ARCTIC CIRCLE IN A CONVERTED LIFEBOAT

THE HIT BEATLES SONG "Yellow Submarine" is the first thing that comes to mind when you see the vessel belonging to English architects Guylee Simmonds and David Schnabel. On closer examination, Stødig is not actually a submarine but a disused lifeboat. Against the icy backdrop of the northern Norwegian landscape, its sunny yellow hue gives it all the appearance of an avant-garde sculpture or a prop from a Wes Anderson film. Originally constructed in Norway in 1997 by Norsafe, prior to being converted, this lifeboat was stored on board a ferry shuttling between Scotland's Western Isles. Robust, unsinkable, and spacious, it was originally designed to carry 100 people in an emergency. Those very properties have now made it the perfect plaything for two bold architects.

Their redesign included the installation of two double cabins at the front, a kitchen with a dining area, a bathroom, two bunkbeds, and a cockpit at the stern. Everything exudes sleek Scandinavian style. For about a year, the two architects (both aged 31) worked part-time on the boat alongside their day jobs as architects, which funded the whole enterprise. The name *Stødig* is a Norwegian adjective that translates roughly as "solid" or "steadfast," honoring the reliable and functional design of the lifeboat. From the very outset, the duo had no intention of leaving their vessel languishing in English waters. As active, adventuresome types, they were keen to head north with their dog, Shackleton. Exploring northern Norway had been Guylee and David's dream long before they decided to embark on this adventure with their converted lifeboat.

Their journey took them to the inland waterways of the Netherlands, into Germany and the Kiel Canal, through Denmark, along the west coast of Sweden, and onward to the final stretch: a three-month summer voyage along the Norwegian coast. As they were limited to the sedate speed of 6 knots (7 mph/11 kph), they dubbed this roughly 3,100 mile (5,000 km) journey "the slow adventure." The leisurely pace suited both of them to a tee; the boat moved so slowly that they could read and eat while steering it and watching the stunning Norwegian coast slip by. The presence of their retriever Shackleton meant that they had to go ashore every day, no matter what the weather. Instead of bucket list-style tourism and stopping at only the best-known places, they would go for strolls wherever they could find a good anchorage. This led to serendipitous discoveries of breathtakingly beautiful scenery and unknown hiking trails.

As the boat has a very short keel and a draught of 32 in (80 cm), it is liable to roll a lot amid rough seas. When crossing the Skagerrak from Sweden to Norway, David and Guylee faced a 13 ft (4 m) swell, which made it difficult to stay on course. The passage was especially nerve-wracking for David, who did not have the benefit of much experience with boats. As time went on, however, both of them learned to trust their floating home and their own abilities to get them through tough conditions. "There can't be many places much safer than a lifeboat," laughs David.

Little did they know that this was only the first of a great many spectacular light shows to come.

There have certainly been a lot of memorable moments along the way. David will never forget the moment that he saw the Northern Lights for the first time, in Fleinvær, south of the Lofoten Islands. Little did they know that this was only the first of a great many spectacular light shows to come. On another occasion, they steered around a promontory in the middle of a storm and spotted a collection of dark spots right ahead of their boat, which they feared were dangerous shallows. But when Guylee entered the cockpit, he realized that these patches were actually a school of orcas that had come closer to the surface beneath the *Stødig*. "Our lifeboat gets us to places that would be difficult to access by land and grants us glimpses of an abundance of wildlife," says Guylee.

Tromsø has now become their home port. Guylee lives in northern Norway all year round, although not always on the boat, while David commutes between the U.K. and Tromsø. While in Tromsø, they spend most of their time in the harbor next to other boat-lifers. Several times a year, they go out on trips lasting several weeks, often to the Lyngen Alps. Depending on the time of year, there is plenty of skiing, trail running, kayaking, hiking, and mountain biking to be had. Even during polar nights when the sun does not rise, they do not let the darkness keep them from getting out and about. Taking a cue from the locals, they use headlamps to light their way up to snowy peaks, then back down again to their boat to warm up beside the wood-burning stove. Neither of them hankers after sunnier climes: "We've fallen in love with these incredible mountains and coastal landscapes," enthuses Guylee. "Norway has so much to offer!"

BOAT FACTS The yellow-painted lifeboat is 38 ft (11.5 m) long and 11 ft (3.3 m) wide. Its interior resembles a boutique hotel and can sleep up to eight. Guylee and David were eager to create a home that would not put any constraints on their day-to-day life or work. The architects had the large, curved window installed to enhance the onboard experience, especially in winter, when Norway has only limited daylight. Condensation is their greatest foe during the colder months. The pair worked with the curves of the *Stødig* to create a spacious seating area that would serve as a natural gathering place on board, with concealed storage space for provisions and ski gear. Power for electrical devices comes from an onshore connection, the boat's solar cells, or the diesel motor, a 30 hp Lister Petter.

In winter, Guylee and David have unspoiled views of fairytale snowy landscapes from their converted lifeboat *Stødig*, like here off Ringvassøya, an idyllic island northwest of Tromsø in northern Norway (previous spread). Anchorage in Brandangersundet, north of the city of Bergen, looking over to the rocky Norwegian coast clad in summery green (right page).

The yellow boat moored to rocks on the islet of Sandøya, southern Norway (this page). Both doors lead to cabins in the bow. The galley is on the right and the eating and working area on the left, with a large glass frontage (right page, top). The spray of the lifeboat against the panoramic Lofoten mountainscape (right page, bottom left). A crew of three: Guylee, David, and Shackleton the dog (right page, bottom right).

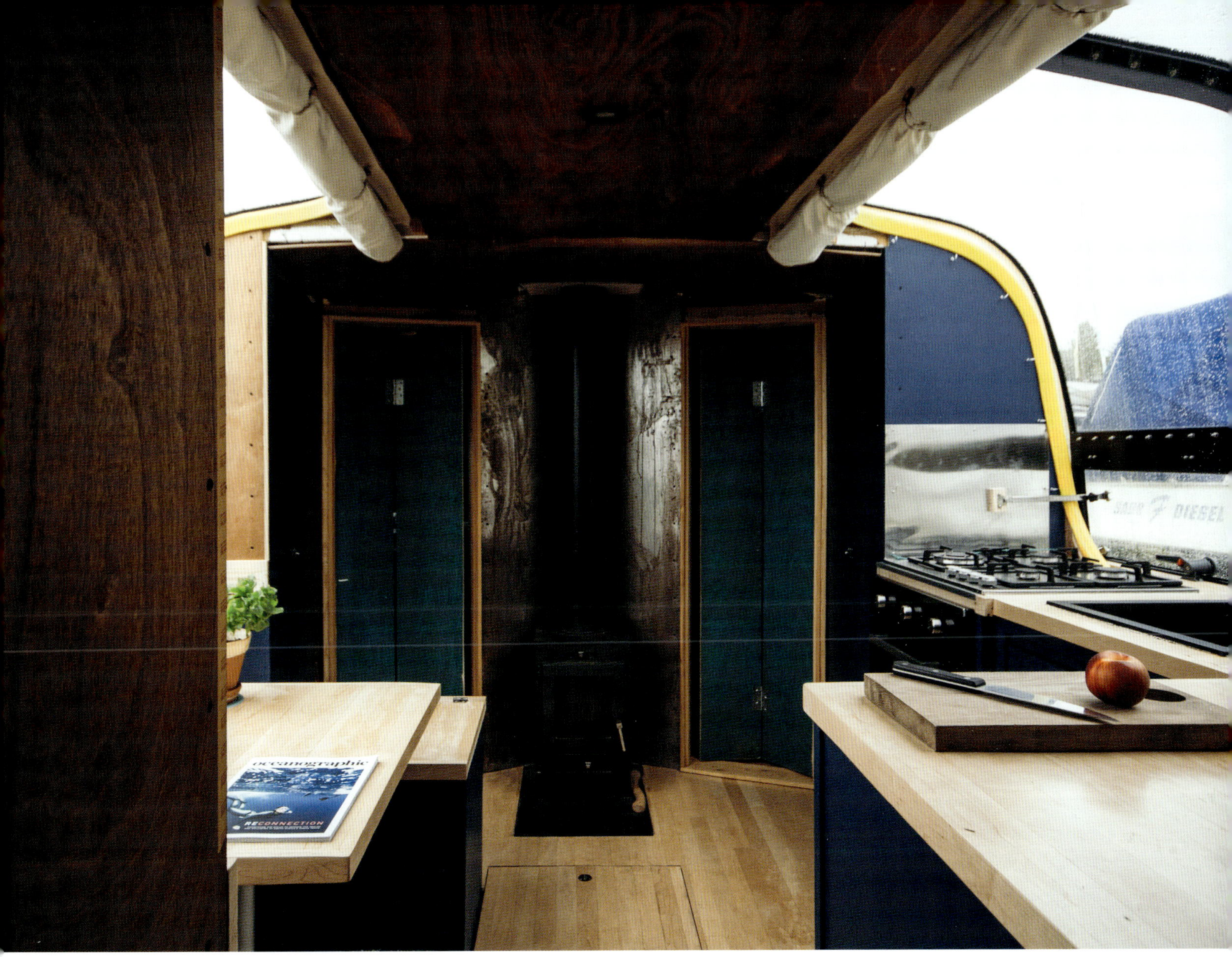
oceanographic
RECONNECTION

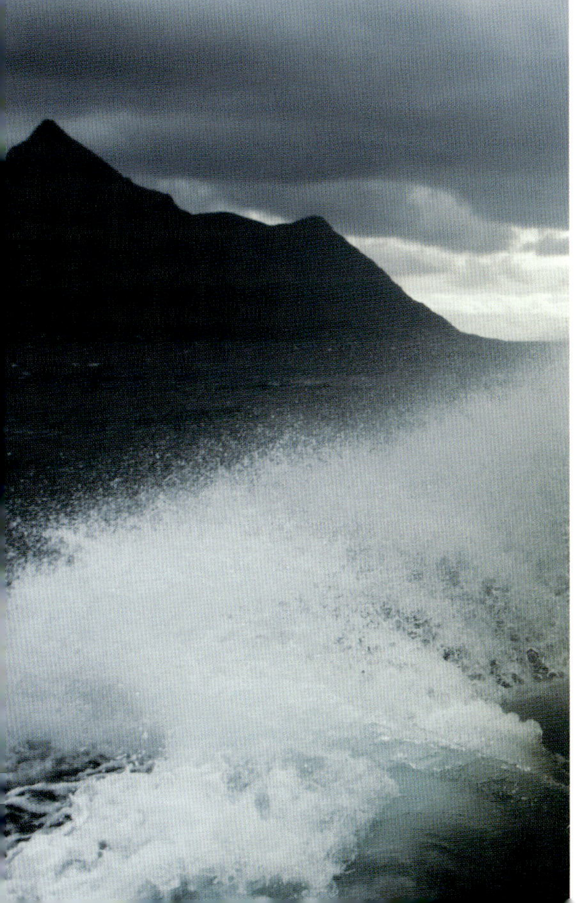

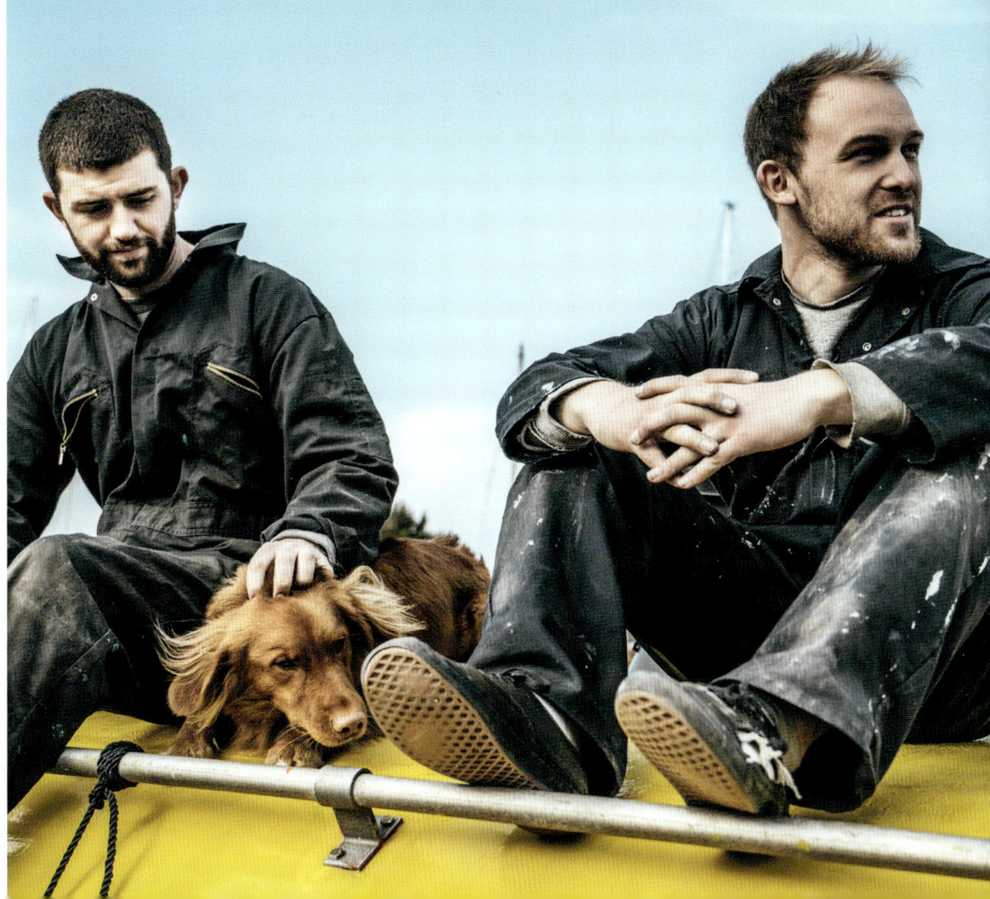

CONQUERING WILD WAVES TO GET TO "THE BIG ICE"

UNIQUE, WILD, and largely cut off from the rest of the world, the white continent of Antarctica is as large as Europe and Greenland combined. Captain Janke Kingma regularly sails with her crew on the three-master *Europa* to the ice-covered area at the South Pole. Sometimes the Dutchwoman steps onto the deck, and it is raining cats and dogs, albeit horizontally because the wind is so brutal—and just a few minutes later, the sun appears, and the wind says goodbye. A few hours later, snowflakes may fall, or massive icebergs may tower over the *Europa,* peeking out from behind thick clouds of fog. At other times, the sturdy steel ship becomes a magnet for penguins, seals, and albatrosses. The 42-year-old also raves about the intense worlds of color that the sky paints over her three-master, which looks tiny in the massive ice universe of Antarctica. Intense blues, soft pinks, and glistening golden yellows merge into paintings, taking up sometimes more, sometimes less space in the sky at hourly intervals.

In 2016, Janke sailed on the bark-rigged sailing vessel for the first time, initially as an officer and now as captain since 2019. She still remembers her first voyage as captain of the *Ocean Wanderer,* as the crew calls the *Europa.* On a Cape to Cape trip—from Ushuaia at the southern tip of South America to Cape Town in South Africa—she was excited and nervous but delighted to be able to put her skills to the test. Janke was born into a family of sailors, and before her time on *Europa,* she sailed in the Atlantic, Pacific, and Arctic Oceans, as well as the Ross Sea. While it is rare for her to encounter other female captains steering large ships across the world's oceans, she has noticed a change. "You don't have to be 6 ft 5 in tall and have a full beard to navigate a big boat—it's not just about physical strength, it's about being a good organizer, and forming and leading teams," Janke says. "As this becomes more deeply embedded in our society, my profession will certainly attract more women," she believes.

Alongside the captain, the international crew of 16 includes a first officer, a bosun, several deckhands, an engineer, a cook, and a doctor. The permanent crew is joined by the "voyage crew," consisting of up to 48 guests, most of whom have no sailing skills but actively participate in the voyage, stumping up a five-figure sum to be on board. These Antarctic expeditions last between 22 and 54 days and take place four to five times during the southern hemisphere's summer season (i.e., between November and March). The shorter cruise departs from Ushuaia and heads directly to Antarctica. Meanwhile, the voyage that lasts almost two months begins in Uruguay, goes to the Falkland Islands and South Georgia, and ends in Antarctica. From there, the ship takes a direct course for the return.

The three-master looks tiny in the massive ice universe of Antarctica.

To sail into the southern polar region, the ship must pass through the notorious Drake Passage, 400 nautical miles (460 mi/740 km) wide and known for its violent storms. The crew calls the passage "Drake Lake" when it is pleasantly calm and "Wild Drake" when the waves tower over the ship at 26 ft (8 m) high. However, there is often little wind for days between low-pressure systems, so the notorious wave crests start to level off. Ice poses a greater risk to the *Europa,* so a radar is deployed to prevent any collisions with drift ice. But the crew keeping ice watch from the foredeck is even more important. Ice lights are used in the dark to improve visibility, and the ship's speed is reduced. Janke spends considerable time studying the wind and weather before and during the long passages and making detailed route plans based on forecasts. She tries to avoid strong low-pressure systems. "We either shelter in a safe place or alter our course," Janke says.

In Antarctica, the three-masted bark moors in sheltered bays, and guests and guides enter the icy landscape almost daily to observe glaciers, seals, and penguin colonies up close. Meanwhile, the crew on board keeps an eye on the weather, which can change with no advance warning. Janke's most magical moments in the icy wilderness include encountering a school of humpback whales eating krill in peaceful silence near the ship's steel hull. Respect for the environment and the oceans plays an important role in the company's philosophy. Research teams or students dedicated to environmental projects can be found on board for longer ocean crossings.

Janke and her crew are among the most awe-inspiring sailors in the world, and yet the captain remains modest: "Of course, it's a great adventure to sail to Antarctica, but for me hiking in a forest in the Netherlands, one I've never visited before, is an adventure, too. Adventures can be big and small," she says. ◄

BOAT FACTS Stepping aboard the *Europa,* you feel like you are on the set of an action movie. The steel boat was built in Hamburg in 1911 and was initially used as a lightship on the River Elbe. In the 1980s and 1990s, it was converted at a shipyard in Amsterdam into an expedition and oceangoing vessel with three masts and bark rigging and has now been sailing the world's oceans as a charter ship under the Dutch flag for over 20 years. The *Europa* is 184 ft (56 m) long 25 ft (7.5 m) wide, has a draft of 13 ft (3.9 m), and is 108 ft (33 m) high. When all her 24 sails are up, the sail area measures 13,455 ft^2 (1,250 m^2). Below deck are heated cabins for the permanent crew and 12 cabins with bunkbeds, each with its own wet room, for up to 48 guests. Cooking is done in the large galley, and the crews dine together in the traditional mahogany deckhouse with a bar. The saloon and the cozy library invite you to read and write logbooks, sea permitting.

The sky aglow: the crew of the *Europa* regularly enjoys astounding natural spectacles in the Antarctic Ocean (right page, top). Researchers often join them on board for longer ocean crossings. Microscopic animals can be caught a plankton net and then examined under a microscope (right page, bottom).

The *Europa* in her element in the Antarctic, surrounded by ice and penguins (left page; this page; next spread, left page, top right; and spread after next). The bark's dog, Boreas, has already accompanied the *Europa* on several long voyages (previous spread, right page, bottom right).

Three captains—Janke Kingma (this page, left and right page, bottom right), Klaas Gaastra (right page, top), and Eric Kesteloo—take it in turns every couple of months to steer the stately three-masted ship on the voyage from Ushuaia, Argentina, through the Drake Passage and onward to Antarctica.

VOYAGING THROUGH THE ICE TO THE CARIBBEAN

WHEN SAILING from Europe to the Caribbean, sailors usually choose the "Barefoot Route" and let the trade winds blow them across the Atlantic past the Canary Islands. Those seeking an even greater adventure choose the route across the Arctic to tropical climes, like photographer Niklas Marc Heinecke and skipper Joscha Brörmann, who were primarily drawn to the solitude. "If you look at the equator, you will see a motorway of sailing boats, but if you look to the north, only a few mad people venture there. And I wanted to be one of them," Niklas laughs.

Niklas, 34, and Joscha, 35, started their trip in Germany in June 2019. They sailed via Norway to the Shetland and Faroe Islands, stopping off in Iceland and Greenland during the summer months, and then continuing their route at the end of August via the Labrador Sea to Canada and the east coast of the United States. After five months, they finally reached the Caribbean after several thousand nautical miles. One or two fellow travelers often accompanied them on their legs to split the costs.

Joscha grew up sailing and regularly takes yachts across the Baltic Sea, the Mediterranean, or back and forth between the Caribbean islands. Niklas obtained a sailing license on an inland waterway in Hamburg only two years before departure. The friends spent one and a half years preparing for their big trip, refitting Joscha's boat and completing safety training. They then spent three months sailing in the Swedish and Estonian Baltic Sea as practice.

What fascinated them most on their Arctic tour was the cold. "Cold air is so clear. It sharpens the contours so far out at sea. You can see for miles, and there's no other person to be seen for miles. It's incredible," Niklas enthuses. Greenland, the largest island on earth, more than 80 percent of which is covered by a thick ice sheet, particularly fascinated the two. "Greenland has no light pollution, no markings, hardly any maps, and almost no traces of people, apart from garbage." In addition, some huge glaciers and mountains rise more than 3,280 ft (1,000 m) above the water. "When you are surrounded by ice, you can hear it crackle constantly, just like the sound of opening a can of Coke," Niklas continues.

When the two were not sailing, and the boat did not need any repairs, they went hiking into the beguiling wilderness. While hiking up a 1,000 ft (300 m) high peak, the crew spotted a humpback whale down in their anchorage, calmly circling the *Ju Mar.* The cruising yacht suddenly looked tiny next to the gigantic marine mammal. They also remember mooring in Aappilattoq. The small Inuit village lies in the Prince Christian Sound on the southern tip of Greenland. On the small peninsula, a few colorful houses huddle between the steep rock faces. After landing with the dinghy, they met the village chief and learned more about the fishing village and its history from him, which—apart from a few cruise ships—rarely receives visitors.

The ever-changing wind speeds, from calm to 45 knots (50 mph/80 kph), and waves up to 26 ft (8 m) high often presented the crew with challenges, and they often had to contend with seasickness on the rough seas. "But there was also something incredibly beautiful about every storm when the sun shone through the breaking crests, and we could watch the terns swooping," Niklas recalls.

When you are surrounded by ice, you can hear it crackle just like the sound of opening a can of Coke.

Joscha's *Ju Mar* is not a classic Arctic sailboat: it is made of fiberglass and therefore offers less protection against ice than a sailboat made of steel or aluminum. To prevent any collisions with drift ice between Iceland and Greenland, the crew members took turns keeping watch every four hours.

After leaving the cold climes behind, they reached Newfoundland after four days of continuous sailing, and they then realized what they had missed along the way: trees! They were able to smell the forests miles from the Canadian coast. A few weeks later, Niklas had the opportunity to fulfill a childhood dream: the adventurers anchored very close to Central Park in New York City and landed with their dinghy directly in Manhattan. In early November, they cast off from New York for the final stretch across the Gulf Stream to Bermuda and sailed into the Caribbean a short time later.

Niklas believes the trip changed him. He got to know himself and his current girlfriend on the first leg and realized how important photography and nature are to him. What surprised him was how content living on a boat made him. "You live in the smallest space, you don't need many material items, and you are happy," he says. If you want to sail this route, you should prepare well, always have a plan B in your pocket, along with a sprinkling of naivete. Niklas and Joscha have just returned from a several-week sailing trip in Svalbard, and Niklas would like to sail to Greenland again soon—this time longer and even farther into the ice.

BOAT FACTS The *Ju Mar* is over 20 years old, 42 ft (13 m) long, and 13 ft (4 m) wide. Bought new, the yacht, manufactured in Germany by the German series producer Bavaria, costs over $212,000 (€200,000). Joscha found a used club boat on an online portal in 2017. The bluewater boat has three berths and two bathrooms with toilets and showers. The friends equipped the boat for their expedition into the ice with 600 W solar panels, a wind generator, a hydro generator, and a desalination system to always have fresh water on board for drinking, cooking, and showering. An induction stovetop was used to prepare meals and coffee, with a diesel auxiliary heating system and heat exchanger on the engine providing homely warmth in the saloon and bunks. They baked their own bread during their trip using a bread maker stored under a bench seat, and a small garden kept below deck supplied them with fresh herbs. In addition to the crew, two sets of kitesurfing equipment, a stand-up paddle board, a skateboard, a fishing rod, and a hammock were kept on board for their travels.

The *Ju Mar* beside an iceberg in the Denmark Strait, a sound between Greenland and Iceland (previous spread). Scrumptious dishes at the start of their voyage in the Baltic Sea (right page, top left). The imposing landscape of ice and glaciers in Greenland never ceased to amaze the crew (next spread). Niklas working on repairs (right page, top right). After their Arctic adventure, they docked in New York City (right page, bottom).

Friends of Niklas came upon a walrus colony while hiking on Svalbard (left page). The *Ju Mar* off the coast of Iceland in summer (this page, right). The crew encountered orcas off the Faroe Islands (next spread, left page, top left). On the Shetland Islands, they met Shetland ponies and sheep (next spread, right page, bottom right and left). In Iceland, they went hiking on the magical Westman Islands (next spread, left page, bottom). The picturesque anchorage at Aappilattoq, Greenland (next spread, right page, top).

GHOST TOWNS AND GLACIERS

INSTEAD OF CLIMBING a classic career ladder after their college degrees, Kika Mevs and Daniel Deckert decided eight years ago to buy a sailboat—without ever having sailed before. "Don't buy a couch if you want to travel the world," someone once said to them when they were at school. "Don't buy a couch" became Kika's and Daniel's life motto. *Uma,* a Pearson 36 from 1972, into which they built a secondhand electric motor, has since been home to the Haitian and the Canadian, who make money from YouTube videos, among other things.

In 2020, they set out on a new adventure in cold climes after sailing the U.S. coast and the Caribbean islands for several years. Their original idea was to cross the North Atlantic via Greenland and Iceland, but the weather had other plans, so the Atlantic crossing ran from Canada to England. From there, they sailed north along the Norwegian coast for a year before spending the summer of 2021 in Svalbard. "Sailing in Norway and Svalbard was one of the biggest but most beautiful challenges we have faced with our *Uma* so far," says Daniel. The cold was the least of their problems, even in the Norwegian winter. The Gulf Stream ensures that the European North Sea does not freeze along most stretches of coastline, so the water temperature was between 26 and 41°F (2 and 5°C), and the temperature in their boat never dropped below freezing—even when it was -4°F (-20°C), outside. The main thing that kept them warm at anchor was their wood-burning stove, which they had installed specifically for this expedition. However, they spent most of the winter nights in various harbors, where they could use their electric heater thanks to onshore power.

Strong currents and downdrafts whizzing along the Norwegian mountains often challenged the crew. "It felt like sailing in 3D winds at times," Daniel recalls. The crossing from Tromsø in northern Norway to Longyearbyen took around four days. "Svalbard is often sold as absolutely isolated. So before we left the Norwegian mainland, we prepared ourselves as if we were sailing to another planet," says Kika. Once there, however, they were surprised by the variety of things on offer: they found the best-stocked supermarket in the northern latitudes, a cinema, a museum, washing machines, restaurants, and good internet reception. However, that changed when they turned their backs on Svalbard's administrative center.

The rugged landscape now looked like someone had placed a monochrome filter in front of their eyes. It was precisely this special charm that the 32- and 34-year-olds immediately fell for. In addition to mooring directly in front of a glacier, they were particularly impressed by the town of Pyramiden, an abandoned miners' settlement on the Billefjorden in Dickson Land. Walking through the ghost town, they felt like they were in a zombie movie. There is only one hotel left in the place—and it was there that they had one of their best encounters: they met a bartender who told them exciting stories about her life in the remote place and thus let them look deeper into the culture and everyday life of the local people.

The rugged landscape looked like someone had placed a monochrome filter in front of their eyes.

In a rather unspectacular bay, they then experienced what many sailors dream of all their lives: after waking up, they discovered three polar bears on a small island next to their boat. Kika and Daniel had heard several times that polar bears sometimes climbed onto smaller sailboats at anchor. So they even took their rifle, which you always have to carry in Svalbard, to their bunk or watch post on deck at night. Their biggest fear, however, was that one of the ice floes could severely damage their hull. Kika and Daniel learned to set the radar to warn them of approaching ice. Most importantly, they kept ice watch from the beginning of July until the end of August. For two months, one of them was always awake. Leaving the boat for longer excursions ashore was now surprisingly unimaginable for the two-person crew. "That was exhausting. A crew of four to six would have been ideal for that time," says Kika.

The *Uma* against the rugged backdrop of Svalbard in summer (previous spread). Kika and Daniel take a chilly dip in Norway (right page). The couple spent five months sailing above the Arctic Circle, mostly in Norwegian waters (spread after next). From Svalbard, the crew sailed on to Iceland (next spread). The *Uma* in the narrow Trollfjord, northern Norway (next spread but one).

But for them, the biggest difference between sailing in the Caribbean and sailing in Norway and Svalbard was in their equipment: in the Caribbean, they did not even possess shoes, while in Norway and Svalbard they constantly lived in their down sweaters and thermal bottoms made of merino wool.

"Eight years ago, when we started sailing, our boat was a means to an end. Over the years, we have become better and better at sailing. But for us, it continues to be the adventure beyond the next horizon that drives us to sail onward," says Daniel. ◀

SAILOR'S NOTES: SAILING WITH AN ELECTRIC MOTOR Electric motors are not yet as common at sea as on the road. Eight years ago, Kika and Daniel spent $3,000 (around €2,800) and bought their monohull with an engine ready for the scrap heap. Instead of a new expensive diesel engine, they installed a used electric motor they found cheaply on eBay. "We don't need a motor to cross the oceans. That's what our sails are for," Daniel says. The couple need only one to maneuver in and out of a harbor. The electric motor is almost silent and needs no maintenance. It also means they are not reliant on fuel and do not pollute the environment. The winter in a high-latitude region proved challenging, both for them and their sustainable upgrade due to the lack of solar energy that normally charges the engine. Once, they were forced to cross a narrow fjord to reach a much-needed power outlet. Since then, they have kept a small gasoline-powered generator on board for charging in emergencies.

BC645387S

zhik

DEN
166

MICRO-ADVENTURE IN A TINY SAILBOAT

IF THE WORLD-FAMOUS HEROINE of the Pippi Longstocking tales had to choose a sailboat, she would perhaps get herself a small Spækhugger and explore Scandinavian waters as she pleases with her monkey, horse, and colorful flag. Just 24½ ft (7.4 m) long and 7½ ft (2.3 m) wide, the Spækhugger named *Gaia* is owned by Sara Lohse and Xan Browne, who both grew up in the U.K. and later fell for the charms of Copenhagen. *Gaia* is moored in the Danish capital's bustling harbor amid a colorful potpourri of sailboats. From there, the 27- and 28-year-olds use their "adventure mobile" mainly in the summer months—for midsummer parties along the city's canals, weekend cruises to the surrounding islands, or trips lasting several weeks to the South Funen Archipelago or Swedish archipelagos. When it comes to big trips, Sara and Xan, who both studied architecture, have one rule: only one travel bag per person is allowed on board. Storage space is scarce on the small sailboat, built in the mid-1970s. The cabin consists of a space without headroom with a small kitchen unit, two hammock-like armchairs made of canvas that the previous owner installed, and a mattress in the bow where Sara and Xan sleep. Up to two guests can also make themselves comfortable in two narrow bunks in the stern—affectionately called "the coffins" by the crew—that can also be converted into storage space. While Sara and Xan cannot imagine living on their yacht year-round, a larger yacht for their alternative lifestyle or a longer trip, including an Atlantic crossing, would be quite conceivable.

Last summer, their longest trip to date took them to the idyllic Gothenburg Archipelago on the west coast of Sweden, which beckons with its overgrown granite rocks, secluded bays, red and yellow wooden cottages, and unspoiled nature. In three weeks, they covered 600 nautical miles (690 mi/1,110 km). One of their stops on their way there was Samsø. The Danish island in the Kattegat is a popular place for yoga retreats and hippies at heart and is celebrated as the world's most environmentally friendly island. Samsø is energy self-sufficient and carbon neutral. Sara and Xan were particularly drawn to the local food and restaurant scene. They encountered sea kale for the first time, which they collected and then fried on board seasoned with sea salt and finished with lemon zest and Parmesan. Since then, the plant, which is a protected species in some other EU countries, has become one of their go-to snacks while sailing. "The coastal landscapes of Denmark and Sweden are quite different from our perspective from the sailboat. Denmark is very flat and has many sandy beaches, while Sweden is rockier and dotted with granite landscapes," Sara explains. In addition to the many small rock islands on the Gothenburg Archipelago, where they moored with shore fasts, they particularly liked the car-free island of Åstol, made of volcanic rock. The harbor has been adapted to the natural shape of the island, with small houses and alleys clustered around it. Sara and Xan are enthusiastic about natural harbors, a typical feature of the Swedish archipelagos. There, unlike dropping anchor in the open sea, their small boat does not become an object of play for the waves as quickly.

On Samsø, they collected sea kale for the first time, which they fried on board.

Their best experience was mooring off the uninhabited island of Romsø, which lies west of Copenhagen in the Great Belt. At the time, they did not possess a dinghy, so they unceremoniously packed their gear into a dry bag and swam through a thick bank of seaweed to shore to explore the island. Later that evening, a group of harbor porpoises circled the *Gaia*. "The bright colors of the sunset were reflected in the water, and their fins unexpectedly pierced the surface," Sara remembers, eyes shining. They experienced similarly magical moments while sailing in light winds with spinnakers and on their first date, sleeping on deck under the stars, then on Xan's grandfather's boat.

But smaller adventures are also possible in boat-friendly Copenhagen for the two sailors, who have been together for four years. Xan still remembers when Sara and her best friend sailed toward him in the middle of Copenhagen. They were out for dinner on a balmy summer evening, and there were many boats in the water. "It looked pretty epic, *Gaia* coming into the old Copenhagen harbor with full sails between the new theater and the opera house," Xan enthuses. For the two, living a simpler life for a month at a time during the year also has an impact on their city life in their apartment. They become more aware of things in their daily lives, such as how much waste they generate each day. "Life on the boat has a therapeutic quality for me," Xan says. "Sometimes I get annoyed that the wind comes from the wrong direction or gets too strong. But instead of getting upset about it, sailing has taught me to enjoy the moment anyway."

SAILOR'S NOTES: COOKING OUTSIDE THE GALLEY Sara and Xan are passionate foodies. They love to cook in the cockpit or outdoors in a bay using their gas stove. They love foraging and trying out edible delicacies from nature. For them, the most important kitchen essentials on board, besides the classics, include an Aeropress for good coffee and a fillet knife to gut freshly caught fish. They have invested in a barbecue and a matching pizza stone to make the perfect boat pizza. Their favorite recipe is smoked shrimp with cherry tomatoes (which they buy when on shore on one of the Danish islands) in a sauce of oranges, butter, garlic, and white wine. They stockpile a large supply of instant noodles below deck for when they have hunger pangs or during stronger swells, and after each port call, the crew rewards themselves with Polish pickles and beer before stopping at a restaurant. They are excited to learn how to ferment and bake bread.

Casting off, bound for Ven: just a few nautical miles northwest of Sara and Xan's home port of Copenhagen lies their go-to island for weekend trips (previous spread). In summer, the couple embarked on a six-week sailing trip from Denmark to the Gothenburg Archipelago (right page).

The crew enjoys exquisite views of their anchorage from the church in the village of Kyrkbacken on the Swedish island of Ven, which lies in the Øresund (this page). From the *Gaia,* Xan surveys the view of the uninhabited island of Romsø in the Great Belt (right page, top left). Sara cooks her signature dish of smoked shrimp in the cockpit (right page, bottom left).

Before Sara and Xan bought the *Gaia,* they sailed the Stockholm Archipelago in a rented sailboat (left page). Sara loves foraging for sea kale on the sustainable island of Samsø (this page, left) and deep-frying it on board. Sara and Xan spent 10 days exploring the Gothenburg Archipelago in their Spaekhugger sailboat (this page, right).

RAUM
SCHIFF

FROM SPEEDBOAT TO SELF-SUFFICIENT "SPACESHIP"

IN A VINTAGE CAMPER VAN, Thea Sparmeier and Moritz Wussow drove through Spain and Morocco for a year. They'd been looking for an alternative living concept and a home of their own where they could express themselves creatively. But life in Moritz's van wasn't for them in the long run, they realized, so they broadened their horizons. Moritz, a boat builder and industrial designer, and Thea, a communication designer, set out to find a ready-made hull that they could customize. They found *K6,* an aluminum speedboat that had been used as a floating conference room for some time, but was now looking for a new purpose—which Thea and Moritz were happy to provide.

"When the water is warmer than the air, we sink into the fog with our *Raumschiff* ('Spaceship'), and it feels like we've just come to Earth from outer space," says Thea. The spacey prototype, welded together by robots at a company based in Duisburg, Germany, had even been a recipient of the Red Dot Design Award in the past. It was perfect for Thea and Moritz's project—a 301 ft^2 (28 m^2) creative playground with exciting outdoor areas.

Overhauling the 46 ft (14 m) long and 13 ft (4 m) wide vessel took 18 months. With the exception of the insulation, the 30- and 33-year-olds planned and built everything themselves. They also made the bulk of the furniture themselves. The boat is divided into four areas: the stern houses is the fully equipped kitchen with a seating area and kitchenette with coffee machine, oven, dishwasher, and washing machine. A passageway leads you to the sleeping berth, the bathroom with separate toilet and shower spaces, and the hearthside room in the bow, with a couch and a pellet stove with warm air distribution. The creative duo have managed to create an airy ambience by installing a folding glass wall, which can be completely pushed to the side, between the kitchen and the terrace at the rear. The floor can be lifted at various points to provide access to the technical and storage space below. In addition, there is a cellar under the kitchen with a drinking water and wastewater tank along with a filter system.

Their home port is Potsdam, southwest of Berlin. Sometimes, they work together remotely from the boat's office, or Thea goes to her studio and Moritz to his workshop. When they travel a bit farther in their converted speedboat, they moor up and look out over Potsdam's skyline at night. If they travel a little farther still, they come to waters surrounded by forests, which they share only with ducks, wild geese, and beavers.

From their floating home Thea and Moritz love experiencing the different seasons in their home state, Brandenburg. When the first rays of sunshine appear in spring, the cherry trees blossom on the shore, and the wildlife awakens around them, they love to jump into the water from the deck with no clothes on. In the summer, they are out on their boat as much as possible, anchored at the same spot for days on end, making pizza with friends in the pizza oven on their roof and sleeping out under the stars, or they go on vacation with other boat-lifers for a few weeks. In the fall, the colorful leaves are reflected in the water, and it becomes cozier and quieter on the River Havel.

They will always remember the moment when they were able to skate around the hull of their boat.

They also enjoy winter on board very much. From the very beginning, they have equipped and insulated their *Raumschiff* to enable them to live on board all year round. "In winter, we are almost alone on the water, because the majority of boats are in winter storage or in the harbor," Thea tells us. However, their solar panels often do not generate enough power in the cold season, so they have to use onshore power in the harbors. Nevertheless, they regularly go out for a night and listen to the waves crashing against their hull in relative seclusion. They will always remember the moment when their ship was surrounded by a 4 in (10 cm) thick layer of ice, and they could walk out onto the ice from their deck and skate around their hull. That same winter was also a dream come true for the crew: when the ice layer was not as thick, they used their aluminum ship as an icebreaker and plowed through a frozen lake with its bow tip. "Many people called us crazy, but our ship managed it, and the experience and scenery were stunningly beautiful," says Thea.

In theory, their engine, which now has only 60 hp instead of the 900 it used to have, could take them at 6 mph (9 kph) along rivers and canals and through numerous locks all the way to the Mediterranean. Next year, however, they would first like to set off for France via the Netherlands and Belgium and work exclusively on board. "We'll probably be traveling for a whole year or more, because the journey should be the destination and we don't know if we'll ever want to stay longer at one spot," Moritz says.

SAILOR'S NOTES: UPCYCLING ONBOARD Thea and Moritz believe that many things deserve a second life and not everything has to be produced from scratch. Accordingly, they used things in their ship that had already been in use or would have ended up on the scrap heap without their intervention. An old trampoline frame was used to create their floating sofa, and they clad the hallway with recycled offset printing plates that reflect the water and create a uniquely atmospheric lighting effect. The round sink in the bathroom is made from an old drainpipe they discovered by the side of the street. They tracked down the owner, who donated it to the creative couple. They made the kitchen table legs from recycled plastic, old kite fabric serves as a shower curtain, and their 10 solar panels could previously be found on a house in Morocco. "Upcycling often means more effort, but it also makes you very happy because each object has its own story," says Thea.

Thea and Moritz on their self-built sofa in the room containing their pellet stove. In the foreground are the mirrored offset printing plates that line the hallway (right page, top). Moritz in the couple's canoe, the *Tschaika* (right page, bottom left). Thea loves jumping into the water from the *Raumschiff* ("Spaceship," a converted speedboat) at any time of year (right page, bottom right).

Sunset beyond the River Havel (this page). The matte-green galley kitchen is fully equipped with a dishwasher, oven, and portafilter machine (right page, top right). The creative couple built the kitchen table themselves (right page, bottom left). In summer, they hold regular pizza parties on their roof (right page, bottom right).

SIEMENS

INDEX

Setting a Course for Freedom

Photography: Hedvig von Essen & Mattias Wernersson @sailingmonkii (p. 4), Axel Hackbarth @endlesssunshinesailors (p. 5), Arnoud Apituley @barkeuropa (p. 6), Nicole Carlsen & Sam Hawkins-Pitman @nicolecarlsen @sam_hawk (p. 7)

Having the Northwestern Mediterranean Coast as Your Front Yard

LA HOLANDESA II
@sailingdmed

Photography: Kirsten Pastijn & Gonzalo de Velasco (pp. 10–17)

Charting a Course for Creativity

KALMOS
@kalmoslebateau

Photography: Coline Amos (pp. 18–25)

One Couple's Quest for Culture and Kitesurfing

BUGANVILIA
@sailingbuganvilia

Photography: Catalina Eyzaguirre & Juan Ignacio Vender lacontramaestre.com (pp. 26–37)

Many Routes Lead into the Great Blue Yonder

Photography: Allison Medeiros & Denis Dowling @_alli_sun_ @capndarling (p. 38), Elena Dostal & Ben Schaschek @elenaundben (p. 39), Axel Hackbarth @endlesssunshinesailors (p. 41)

From Van-Life to Boat-Life

KALA
@lucafroehlingsdorf

Photography: Luca Froehlingsdorf lucafroehlingsdorf.com (p. 42, p. 46 top left & bottom, p. 47 top & bottom left, p. 49), Ricardo Brüning (pp. 45, 48), Claudius Brünn (p. 46 top right), Katharina Ursinus (p. 47 bottom right)

Taking the Slow Route to Hawaii by Catamaran

OHANA
@elenaundben

Photography: Elena Dostal & Ben Schaschek elenaundben.de (pp. 50–55)

Between Butterflies and Soul Food in the Turkish Aegean

SEA SOUL
@seasouldiary

Photography: Kristina Avdeeva & Niko Tsarev (pp. 56–61)

From Sweden to the Caribbean and Back as a Mature Gap Year

MONKII
@sailingmonkii

Photography: Hedvig von Essen & Mattias Wernersson (pp. 64–69)

Steering a Course between Rays and Remote Working

NAVIKA
@navika_sailing

Photography: Alexandra Lakin & Lars Sandved navika.earth (pp. 70–77)

Zigzagging Their Way from the U.K. to Guadeloupe

ADHARA
@sailingadhara

Photography: Jessica Schoeller-Szüts & Jan-Hendryk Büse sailingadhara.com (pp. 78–87)

Diving into an Island Paradise

Photography: Nicole Carlsen & Sam Hawkins-Pitman @nicolecarlsen @sam_hawk (p. 88), Jessica Schoeller-Szüts & Jan-Hendryk Büse @sailingadhara (p. 89, 91), Alexandra Lakin & Lars Sandved @navika_sailing (p. 90)

Sailing the Route Less Traveled

AMANZI
@sailing.on.amanzi

Photography: Jason Beaufort, Clara Di Prima & Nicholas Gasser patreon.com/sailingonamanzi (pp. 92–101)

Sailing the Scottish Hebrides in a Cutter

EDA FRANDSEN
@edafrandsen_sailing
@_stellamarina___

Photography: Stella Marina Stabbins stella-marina.co.uk, Eda Frandsen Sailing Ltd eda-frandsen.co.uk (pp. 102–107)

A Life at Sea in Perpetuity

MR. BADGER
@_alli_sun_
@capndarling

Photography: Allison Medeiros & Denis Dowling littleschoonerstudiop.com (pp. 108–113)

California Dreaming Aboard a Self-Built Wooden Cutter

MAYFLY
@nate_stephensonn

Photography: Nate Stephenson Photography (pp. 116–123)

Following the "Barefoot Route" from Norway to New Zealand

BEAVER
@nicolecarlsen
@sam_hawk

Photography: Nicole Carlsen & Sam Hawkins-Pitman sailingbeaver.com (pp. 124–131)

Adventures in the Kingdom of the Humpback Whale

AGÁPĒ
@voyagesofagape

Photography: Rachel Moore & Joshua Shankle voyagesofagape.com (pp. 132–143)

Learning to Live With Less at Sea

Photography: Allison Medeiros & Denis Dowling @_alli_sun_ @capndarling (p. 144), Lily Mercieca & Hayden Greener @thegreenertwo (p. 146 top left), Alexandra Lakin & Lars Sandved @navika_sailing (p. 146 bottom right), Liz Clark @captainlizclark (p. 147)

Sailing among Coral Reefs and Crocodiles

HAVEN
@thegreenertwo

Photography: Lily Mercieca & Hayden Greener thegreenertwo.com (pp. 148–155)

From Solo Sailor to Environmental Activist

SWELL
@captainlizclark

Photography: Liz Clark swellvoyage.com (pp. 156–161)

From British Columbia to the Shores of Mexico

FOOTLOOSE
@fromsnowtosail

Photography: Kayleen VanderRee (p. 162, p. 167 bottom, 168-169), Abby Cooper (p. 165), Sylvia Watkins (p. 166 top), Tyler Turner (p. 166 bottom, p. 167 top)

A Family and Their Greenland Wilderness Adventure Playground

LIFESONG
@lifesongsailing

Photography: Paul-Marie Dorsaz (pp. 172, 176–177), Laurent Marol (p. 175), Pierre Ligonie (p. 178), Christophe Votat lifesongsailing.com (p. 179)

Midwinter to Midsummer to the North Cape

ZEST
@endlesssunshinesailors
@katharina.charpian

Photography: Katharina Charpian katharinacharpian.de & Axel Hackbarth (pp. 180–187)

Adventures in the Land of the Orcas, Northern Lights, and Snowy Peaks

MAKAIRA II
@marinewide

Photography: David González Buendía (p. 188, p. 191 bottom, pp. 196–197), Ismaele Tortella (pp. 192–193, p. 196 bottom left), Sigurd Salberg/MarineWide AS marinewide.com (p. 191 top, p. 195, p. 196 top & bottom right)

Adventures beyond the Arctic Circle

Photography: David González Buendía @marinewide (p. 198), Arnoud Apituley @barkeuropa (p. 200 top left), Laurent Marol @lifesongsailing (p. 200 bottom right), Niklas Marc Heinecke @sailingnaked (p. 201)

Crossing the Arctic Circle in a Converted Lifeboat

STØDIG
@arcticlifeboat

Photography: Guylee Simmonds (p. 202), David Schnabel (pp. 205–206, p. 207 top & bottom left), Luke Taylor arctic-lifeboat.com (p. 207 bottom right)

Conquering Wild Waves to Get to "The Big Ice"

EUROPA
@barkeuropa

Photography:Arnoud Apituley @arnoudap (pp. 208–219)

Voyaging through the Ice to the Caribbean

JU MAR
@sailingnaked

Photography: Niklas Marc Heinecke niklasheinecke.com (pp. 220–229)

Ghost Towns and Glaciers

UMA
@sailinguma

Photography: Kika Mevs & Daniel Deckert sailinguma.com (pp. 230–239)

Micro-Adventure in a Tiny Sailboat

GAIA
@cookinginthecockpit

Photography: Jonas Larsen (p. 240), Sara Lohse (pp. 243–244, p. 245 top & bottom right, p. 246, p. 247 right), Xan Browne (p. 245 bottom left, p. 247 left)

From Speedboat to Self-Sufficient "Spaceship"

RAUMSCHIFF
@raum.schiff

Photography: Manuela Clemens (pp. 248–251, p. 253 top & bottom right), Hannes Schulze (p. 252), Studio Raumschiff raumschiff.studio (p. 253 bottom left)

BOATLIFE

Exploring the Freedom of Maritime Living

This book was conceived, edited, and designed by gestalten.

Edited by ROBERT KLANTEN and ANNA DIEKMANN
Contributing editor: KATHARINA CHARPIAN
Editorial support by EFFIE EFTHYMIADI

Written by KATHARINA CHARPIAN
Translation from German to English by MAISIE MUSGRAVE and LUCIE GALLEN
in association with First Edition Translations Ltd, Cambridge, U.K.

Maps by LUCY ENGELMAN

Editorial management by ANNA DIEKMANN

Design and Layout by JOANA SOBRAL

Photo editor: MADELINE DUDLEY-YATES

Typefaces: Neue Kabel by MARC SCHÜTZ and Marydale by BRIAN WILLSON

Cover image by ROXANNA SEARS/@sailingsonder

Production management by Martin Bretschneider

Printed by Finidr, s.r.o., Český Těšín
Made in Europe

Published by gestalten, Berlin 2023
ISBN 978-3-96704-099-9

3rd printing, 2026

For more information, and to order books, please visit www.gestalten.com

Die Gestalten Verlag GmbH & Co. KG
Mariannenstrasse 9–10
10999 Berlin, Germany
hello@gestalten.com

Bibliographic information published by the Deutsche Nationalbibliothek.
The Deutsche Nationalbibliothek lists this publication in the Deutsche Nationalbibliografie; detailed bibliographic data is available online at www.dnb.de

None of the content in this book was published in exchange for payment by commercial parties or designers; gestalten selected all included work based solely on its artistic merit.

This book was printed on paper certified according to the standards of the FSC®.